Marcomannic Wars AD 165–180

Barbarian Warrior
VERSUS
Roman Legionary

Murray Dahm

Illustrated by Giuseppe Rava

OSPREY PUBLISHING
Bloomsbury Publishing Plc
Kemp House, Chawley Park, Cumnor Hill, Oxford OX2 9PH, UK
29 Earlsfort Terrace, Dublin 2, Ireland
1385 Broadway, 5th Floor, New York, NY 10018, USA
E-mail: info@ospreypublishing.com
www.ospreypublishing.com

OSPREY is a trademark of Osprey Publishing Ltd

First published in Great Britain in 2024

A catalogue record for this book is available from the British Library.

ISBN: PB 9781472858061; eBook 9781472858054;
ePDF 9781472858078; XML 9781472858085

24 25 26 27 28   10 9 8 7 6 5 4 3 2 1

Maps by www.bounford.com
Index by Rob Munro
Typeset by PDQ Digital Media Solutions, Bungay, UK
Printed and bound in India by Replika Press Private Ltd.

Osprey Publishing supports the Woodland Trust, the UK's leading
woodland conservation charity.

To find out more about our authors and books visit
www.ospreypublishing.com. Here you will find extracts, author
interviews, details of forthcoming events and the option to sign up for
our newsletter.

Acknowledgement
I wish to thank both Jona Lendering and Martijn Wijnhoven for their
assistance with photography.

Author's note
Whereas in former periods we have a wealth of surviving written sources
that go into great detail, much less survives intact for our period of
study. Such detailed sources were still being written, but often they are
no more than the names of authors in the surviving record. Moreover,
those sources that do survive, such as Cassius Dio and the *SHA*, are
either fragmentary or unreliable. Nevertheless, they are all we have. On
occasion (and the wars of Marcus Aurelius are one such instance) we find
sources which would, in more abundant literary times, be considered
peripheral now take on a much greater importance because they offer
information and insights lacking in our other surviving sources.

Artist's note
Readers may care to note that the original paintings from which the
colour plates in this book were prepared are available for private sale.
All reproduction copyright whatsoever is retained by the publishers. All
enquiries should be addressed to:

info@g-rava.it

The publishers regret that they can enter into no correspondence upon
this matter.

CONTENTS

Introduction

This bronze figurine of a bound Germanic tribesman dates from the 2nd century AD. He wears his hair in a Suebian knot; the Suebi were the northern neighbours of the Marcomanni, although some warriors are depicted on contemporary monuments with similar knots. (Gryffindor/Wikimedia/CC BY-SA 3.0)

Almost as soon as the brother emperors Marcus Aurelius and Lucius Verus came to power in March AD 161, the Roman Empire was racked by a series of military crises. War was threatening in Britain, the Parthians invaded Armenia and the Germanic tribes of the Chatti and the Chauci invaded Germania Superior and Raetia. The British threat was dealt with by subordinates and the Parthian War (161–66) was prosecuted successfully by Verus. The German frontier would, however, require greater effort. Compounding the problem was the fact that several garrisons on the Rhine and Danube were weakened by sending troops to fight in the Parthian War, making those provinces appear even more tempting. In 166, war was again threatening and several peoples posed threats – especially the Germanic Marcomanni and Quadi, as well as the Sarmatian Iazyges. In Latin the war to subdue them was known as the *bellum Germanicum et Sarmaticum* (German and Sarmatian War). The conflict would occupy Marcus Aurelius and his subordinates until the emperor's death in 180.

The first invasions by the Chatti and Chauci continued until 165, but were not the priority for the Romans; the Parthian War was still under way that year. In October 166, a Triumph was celebrated for the Parthian War, but new invaders in the north were already running amok. It would take some 13 months for the legions and vexillations seconded for the Parthian campaign to return to their home bases. In 166 or 167 new tribes, the Langobardi and Obii, invaded Pannonia. This invasion was repulsed by Roman forces and a truce was arranged, harnessing the skills of the Marcomannic king, Ballomar (or Ballomarius). At the same time or soon after, the Lacringi invaded and an invasion of Dacia was undertaken by a tribe of the Vandals – the Astingi – and the Iazyges. This invasion succeeded in defeating the Roman garrison and killing the governor. In the spring of 168 both emperors, Marcus Aurelius and Lucius Verus, advanced to Aquileia (near modern-day Trieste, Italy) to prepare for an expedition, including the raising of two new legions. Another

invasion, this time by the Marcomanni and the Victuali (aka Victohali and several other spellings), invaded Pannonia.

In January 169, Lucius Verus died and Marcus Aurelius was left to conduct the war alone. He returned to Rome to bury his brother and set out later in the year intending first to subdue the Iazyges, but they defeated the governor of Moesia Inferior and more tribes took the opportunity of this distraction to invade into Germania Superior. Having formed a coalition of tribes, Ballomar ravaged Pannonia and Noricum, defeating the *legio XIIII Gemina Martia Victrix* at Carnuntum (near Petronell-Carnuntum and Bad Deutsch-Altenburg, Austria) and then moved to invade Italy, sacking Opitergium (modern-day Oderzo) and putting Aquileia under siege.

Marcus appointed several new commands and organized the defence of Italy. The siege of Aquileia was raised and the invasion was entirely repulsed by 171. In early 172 another expedition was made against the Iazyges, which saw the dramatic 'Battle on the Ice' on the frozen Danube River that persuaded them to sue for peace – an offer that was rejected by the Romans. Diplomatic efforts saw peace treaties made with other former enemies and some tribes were even enrolled as Roman allies for the forthcoming expedition across the Danube. Later in 172, a Roman invasion across the Danube into Marcomannic territory was conducted, which defeated the Germanic tribe and their allies. From this date, Marcus began using the title *Germanicus* and issuing coins with the legend *Germania Capta* ('Germany captured').

The invasion continued in 173 and 174 against the Quadi, allies of the Marcomanni. During this invasion, one of Marcus' legions, the *legio XII Fulminata*, was surrounded but rescued by the 'Miracle of the Rain', which allowed the Romans to gain the victory. Another Roman invasion of Quadi territory followed in 174 or 175 and the Quadi sued for peace, even ousting their king, Furtius, and installing another. The subjugation was almost complete by the end of the year. The Marcomanni, Quadi and others were enlisted in the Roman Army as auxiliaries. In 175, peace was also made with the Iazyges.

The 160s saw a series of invasions of Roman territory along the Danube River frontier. Several, such as incursions by the Chatti and the Chauci into Germania Superior and Raetia, were not deemed serious enough by the Romans to warrant personal imperial attention. All that changed in 166, however, when the Langobardi and Obii invaded Pannonia Superior. A truce was organized with 11 tribes and Ballomar (or Ballomarius) of the Marcomanni was chosen to represent the Germanic peoples. Another invasion was undertaken, this time by the Lacringi and Astingi, and the Iazyges invaded the province of Dacia, killing the governor.

Marcus Aurelius and Lucius Verus determined to go to the front and departed for Aquileia (near modern-day Trieste, Italy) in 168. The Marcomanni and the Victuali then invaded Pannonia again, but turned about at the approach of the Roman forces. The death of Verus in January 169 gave more tribes the opportunity to invade, crossing into Germania Superior, and the Iazyges invaded Moesia Inferior, killing the governor.

In 170, the Marcomanni and their allies invaded and advanced to Aquileia and Opitergium (modern-day Oderzo, Italy), sacking the latter, the first invasion of Italy in almost 300 years. The Roman garrison at Carnuntum (near Petronell-Carnuntum and Bad Deutsch-Altenburg, Austria) was severely defeated. The same year may also have seen an invasion by the Costoboci, ravaging the Balkans, and reaching the provinces of Moesia, Macedonia and even Achaea (getting as far as Athens itself). In fact, we have multiple invasions listed in the sources by all manner of tribes, on some of which we have only vague information. The Roman response eventually came, probably from Sirmium (modern-day Sremska Mitrovica, Serbia) on the Save (or Sava) River or from Singidunum (modern-day Belgrade, Serbia). Elsewhere, several governors were killed in their attempts to repulse the invasions.

With the raiders expelled, in early 172, a raid by the Iazyges was defeated on the frozen Danube River, probably near Aquincum (modern-day Budapest, Hungary) or perhaps near the Granua River (the modern-day Hron, Slovakia). In the campaigning season of 172, Marcus crossed the Danube into the territory of the Marcomanni and Quadi and, by the end of the year had earned the title *Germanicus*.

Further Roman punitive invasions continued in 173 and 174 against allies of the Marcomanni, the Naristi (or Narisci, or Varisci) and the Quadi. Peace was made and the Iazyges followed suit in 175 after a Roman expedition into their heartland. The Lacringi and Astingi became Roman allies and contingents from the Marcomanni, Quadi and Sarmatian Iazyges were made auxiliaries. In those years there were other invasions too: the Chatti and Hermunduri attempted to cross the Rhine River, but were repulsed, and the Chauci raided the coast of Belgica, bypassing Germania Inferior.

Marcus may have intended to turn the territory of the Marcomanni, Quadi and Iazyges into Roman provinces, but he was distracted in 175 by news of a usurper in the East (the governor and general Avidius Cassius) and marched his army to quell the rebellion. When he returned to the West in late 176, the northern frontier was soon again in turmoil. In 177 the Quadi rebelled, followed by the Marcomanni, and new Roman expeditions were sent to punish them; this time, garrisons were installed in their territory. Marcus was still waging this war when he died in March 180.

Before the newly pacified regions could be made into provinces, however, an urgent distraction occurred in the East. The trusted governor and general Avidius Cassius usurped the throne and Marcus marched to defeat him, even taking the new Marcomannic, Quadi and Iazygian auxiliaries with him to do so. Avidius Cassius was quickly defeated, but Marcus needed to be seen in the East so took his time to head back to Italy and returned to Rome only in late 176. Despite this victory, war would erupt again on the Danube frontier and require further campaigns from August 178 until Marcus' death on the frontier in March 180.

Although our surviving written sources are less plentiful and reliable than we would hope, we also have a remarkable visual record of the war presented on the Column of Marcus Aurelius in the Piazza Colonna, Rome. Less famous than Trajan's Column, Marcus' column nevertheless offers intricate and remarkable detail of uniforms, weapons and narratives of events of the war (for instance the Miracle of the Rain is unmistakable). Using this and other sources from a wide (and sometimes unusual) spectrum, the Marcomannic Wars of Marcus Aurelius can be illuminated in remarkable and vivid detail.

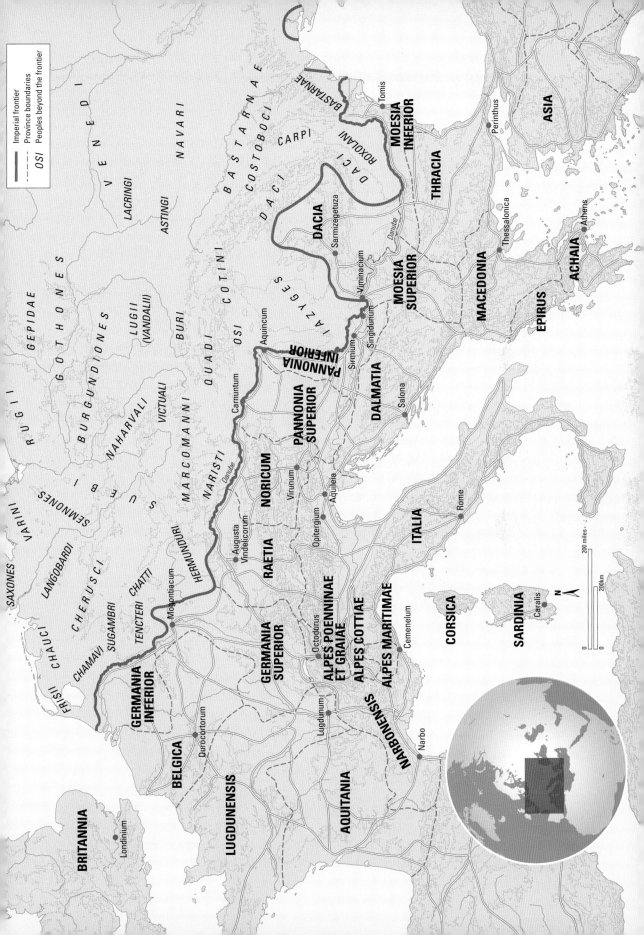

Legend

- Imperial frontier
- Province boundaries
- Peoples beyond the frontier
- *OSI*

Peoples beyond the frontier

SAXONES
VARINI
FRISII
CHAUCI
CHAMAVI
SUGAMBRI
TENCTERI
CHATTI
CHERUSCI
LANGOBARDI
SEMNONES
VENEDI
NAVARI
LACRINGI
ASTINGI
BASTARNAE
COSTOBOCI
CARPI
DACI
ROXOLANI
GEPIDAE
GOTHONES
RUGII
LUGII (VANDALII)
BURI
BURGUNDIONES
NAHARVALI
VICTUALI
MARCOMANNI
NARISTI
QUADI
COTINI
OSI
SUEBI
HERMUNDURI
IAZYGES

Provinces

BRITANNIA
LUGDUNENSIS
BELGICA
AQUITANIA
NARBONENSIS
GERMANIA INFERIOR
GERMANIA SUPERIOR
RAETIA
ALPES POENNINAE ET GRAIAE
ALPES COTTIAE
ALPES MARITIMAE
NORICUM
PANNONIA SUPERIOR
PANNONIA INFERIOR
DALMATIA
DACIA
MOESIA SUPERIOR
MOESIA INFERIOR
THRACIA
MACEDONIA
EPIRUS
ACHAIA
ASIA
ITALIA
CORSICA
SARDINIA

Places

Londinium
Durocortorum
Lugdunum
Narbo
Mogontiacum
Octodurus
Augusta Vindelicorum
Opitergium
Virunum
Aquileia
Carnuntum
Aquincum
Sirmium
Singidunum
Viminacium
Sarmizegetuza
Salona
Tomis
Perinthus
Thessalonica
Athens
Rome
Cemenelum
Caralis

Danube

N

200 miles
200km

The Opposing Sides

ARMY COMPOSITION, RECRUITMENT AND MOTIVATION

Barbarian

In perhaps the most important and influential passage of his ethnographical treatise on Germania written in AD 98, Tacitus gives a description of the Germanic way of making war:

> When they go into battle, it is a disgrace for the chief to be surpassed in valour, a disgrace for his followers not to equal the valour of the chief. And it is an infamy and a reproach for life to have survived the chief, and returned from the field. To defend, to protect him, to ascribe one's own brave deeds to his renown, is the height of loyalty. The chief fights for victory; his vassals fight for their chief. (*Germania* 14)

In a broad sense, this description can be used of the tribesmen of the Marcomanni, Quadi and other peoples. Although the overall accuracy of this description has been questioned, we do find later Germanic cultures following

A view of one of the side panels of the Piccolo Ludovisi Sarcophagus, showing a Roman cavalryman fighting against three naked barbarians. Again, there is the detail (unnecessary if this is a purely idealized scene) of the curved *sica* blade; the enemy shields are geometrically varied, as they are in more 'trustworthy' depictions. The details of the interior of the enemy shield may also be useful (and can be seen on other depictions too). The idea of the Romans' opponents massively outnumbering the imperial forces is also suggested here, more so than on the front panel. (Sailko/Wikimedia/CC BY-SA 3.0)

this very practice, known as the *comitatus* warrior code. Tacitus also surmises a broad organization of tribal warfare: warriors fought for a chief and they, in turn, provided men for a higher chief, all the way to the king.

We do not have any other knowledge of the organization of Germanic armies save for the description of 74 dragon standards (*dracones*) in the (spurious) letter appended to *The First Apology of Justin Martyr* for the Miracle of the Rain in 174. That letter might suggest 74 tribes or subdivisions within an army, although not how they were organized; this letter is discussed in detail below. Usually, however, we are told only of peoples or a horde (sometimes identified in our sources by a single tribe name even when a polyglot alliance) who invaded and plundered before returning across the Danube.

The other side panel of the Piccolo Ludovisi Sarcophagus also depicts naked tribesmen, with accurate details of weapons and shields. We can also note the combined infantry and cavalry action against the Roman cavalryman; here, he is only outnumbered two to one. Unlike his Roman counterpart, the tribesman rides bareback, perhaps reinforcing the idea in the surviving literary accounts that barbarian cavalry were lighter on the ice. Note the quiver hanging from the tree at far left. (Sailko/Wikimedia/CC BY-SA 3.0)

This warrior, one of those surrounding the Roman garrison of Carnuntum, is highly motivated, confident and well-armed. He taunts and jeers his Roman enemies before closing in for the kill.

Weapons, dress and equipment

Our warrior wields a spear (**1**), an important sign of manhood among his people. He is also armed with an axe (**2**), tucked into his belt. He carries a hexagonal shield (**3**) made of wooden boards with a central grip (**4**). His shield has a typical boss and decoration as depicted on various Roman monuments and coins.

The man is bare-headed and wears a beard, a sign that he is a mature warrior. He is clad in a typical long tunic (**5**), trousers (**6**) and shoes (**7**) based on the finds at Thorsberg Moor (Süderbrarup, Germany). Although all Roman depictions of the Marcomanni and other Germanic tribesmen show them unarmoured, we know from the archaeological record that some did wear mail armour (**8**); the mail worn by this warrior is based on the 2nd–3rd-century AD find at Vimose in Denmark. He carries personal effects in a pouch (**9**) on his belt.

This bronze of a kneeling German tribesman dates from the 1st or 2nd century AD. Where it was first unearthed is not recorded, but it was discovered in the Bibliothèque nationale de France in Paris during the late 19th century (Cabinet des Médailles Paris, Inv. No. 915). He wears a Suebian knot and kneels, probably in submission (an alternative argument is that he is depicted praying). He is, however, fully clothed in trousers, tunic and cloak. Tacitus describes the knot in his chapter on the Suebi: 'A national peculiarity with them is to twist their hair back, and fasten it in a knot. This distinguishes the Suevi from the other Germans, as it also does their own freeborn from their slaves. With other tribes, either from some connection with the Suevic race, or, as often happens, from imitation, the practice is an occasional one, and restricted to youth. The Suevi, till their heads are grey, affect the fashion of drawing back their unkempt locks, and often they are knotted on the very top of the head' (Germania 38). (Bullenwächter/Wikimedia/ CC BY 3.0)

Elsewhere, Tacitus characterized the Germanic peoples as a whole as being 'averse to peace', and he pointed out that if a tribe was too long at peace, its youths would voluntarily seek out those tribes who were waging war in order to 'win renown more readily in the midst of peril' (Germania 14). What is more, minor – and major – chieftains could not 'maintain a numerous following except by violence and war' – 'men look to the liberality of their chief for their war-horse and their blood-stained and victorious lance' (Germania 14). The pursuit of plunder and raiding were considered far superior pursuits to ploughing or labouring in a field. The raids over the Danube during Marcus' reign would certainly suggest that several of these traits, although they seem superficial and gross generalizations, remained a broadly accurate summary of many tribes' behaviours towards the 'civilized' and wealthy Roman provinces across the river. In an earlier chapter, Tacitus describes how warriors attached themselves to 'men of mature strength and of long approved valour' (Germania 13). Noting that the followers then competed with one another to be first in the eyes of their chief and 'the chiefs as to who shall have the most numerous and the bravest followers', Tacitus continues:

> it is an honour as well as a source of strength to be thus always surrounded by a large body of picked youths; it is an ornament in peace and a defence in war. And not only in his own tribe but also in the neighbouring states it is the renown and glory of a chief to be distinguished for the number and valour of his followers, for such a man is courted by embassies, is honoured with presents, and the very prestige of his name often settles a war. (Germania 13)

We can, perhaps see this rationale in Ballomar of the Marcomanni being chosen to represent the 11 tribes in the late 160s: he was the strongest and therefore all the others deferred to him.

There are clear indications that the various peoples were considered indistinct from one another, at least to Roman eyes. When Marcus was preparing for his invasion of Marcomannic territory in 171, he made peace with the Quadi, but did not allow them permission to attend the markets. The reason for this, according to the historian Cassius Dio, was 'for fear that the Iazyges and the Marcomanni, whom they had sworn not to receive nor to allow to pass through their country, should mingle with them, and passing themselves off for Quadi, should reconnoitre the Roman positions and purchase provisions' (71/72.3.11). An individual of the Marcomanni or Iazyges could pass himself off as a man of the Quadi with ease.

It would seem that every man of age would fight and would continue fighting into old age. We are even told of women fighting in the ranks with the men (Dio, 71/72.3.2). The idea of numbers in the tribes is very difficult to ascertain, however, and the sources for Marcus' wars do not give us such details very often.

Looking at the attention to detail in this Roman victory trophy made up of enemy equipment, it is difficult to believe that these are not modelled on real items. Several such items may have been brought back to Rome for the eventual Triumph. Note the *dracones*, the ornate shields and the eagle-handled sword on its baldric. (Folegandros/Wikimedia/CC BY-SA 3.0)

This bust of Marcus Aurelius, currently in the Musée Saint-Raymond, Toulouse (RA 61 b), was originally found at the Roman villa of Chiragan (Martres-Tolosane, France). As usual with an imperial command led by men deficient in military experience, several veteran commanders served alongside the emperor during the Marcomannic Wars. For Marcus, in addition to Furius Victorinus, these included Aufidius Victorinus, Vitrasius Pollio, Pontius Laelianus and Dasumius Tullius Tuscus, the last two former governors of Pannonia Superior. Another was Claudius Fronto, who had been with Verus in the East and was made governor of Moesia Superior. The presence of these men on the campaign is preserved through inscriptions (see Birley 1987: 155–56). Furius Victorinus was replaced by two men, M. Bassaeus Rufus and M. Macrinus Vindex (probably the son of the cavalry commander Marcus Vindex mentioned in 166). (Daniel Martin/Wikimedia/CC BY-SA 4.0)

Roman

Owing to various factors, especially the plague Lucius Verus' army brought back from the East in 165 – probably from Seleucia (modern-day Baghdad, Iraq) – the Roman Empire and its armies suffered immensely. This led to an acute manpower shortage. According to the *Scriptores Historiae Augustae* (*SHA*), a series of biographies of emperors from Hadrian to Numerianus, Marcus:

> trained slaves for military service – just as had been done in the Punic war – whom he called Volunteers after the example of the Volones [the name applied to the 8,000 slaves who volunteered to fight for Rome after the defeat at Cannae in 216 BC]. He armed gladiators also, calling them the Compliant (*obsequentes*), and turned even the bandits of Dalmatia and Dardania into soldiers. He armed the Diogmitae [the military police in Greek cities], besides, and even hired auxiliaries from among the Germans for service against Germans. And besides all this, he proceeded with all care to enrol legions for the Marcomannic and German war. (*Marcus* 21.6–8)

These measures suggest a deep manpower crisis at the outset of the Marcomannic Wars, one almost unprecedented in Rome's history. Later historians tell us (Eutropius, *Breviarium* 8.12; Orosius, *History* 7.15.5–6) of whole armies lost to the plague and the greatest doctor of the age, Galen of Pergamon, also tells us of the losses (9.6, 19.18–19). The new legions were the *legio II Pia* and *legio III Concordia* – although later they were renamed *II Italica* and *III Italica* – with the symbols of the she-wolf and twins and stork respectively. The *legio VI Claudia*, stationed in Moesia Superior at Viminacium (near modern-day Kostolac, Serbia), had to enlist twice the normal intake of recruits in 169: 240 replacements (*CIL* 3.14507; Birley 1987: 159). One obvious downside to this was that the newly recruited men lacked the experience of warfare and this, perhaps, shows in their fortunes against the invaders in 170.

COMBAT

Legionary, *legio XIIII Gemina Martia Victrix*

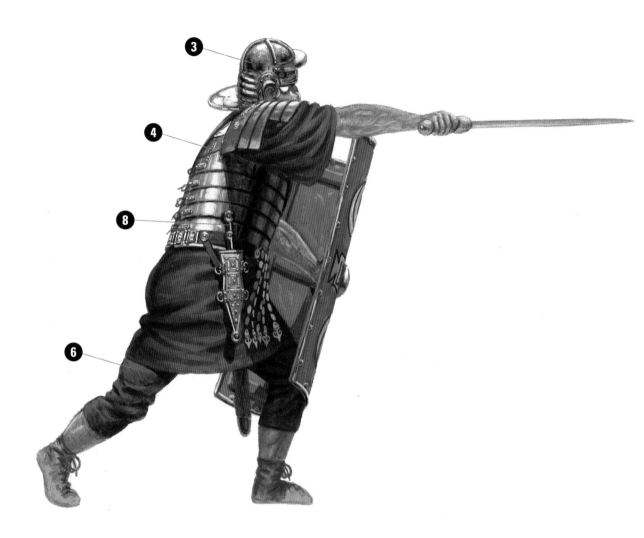

Newly recruited, this young legionary of the *legio XIIII Gemina Martia Victrix* has marched out from his base at Carnuntum with vexillations of other legions and auxiliary troops to face the invading Marcomanni. Even though the Romans have 20,000 men they are massively outnumbered; he and his companions face annihilation, prompting fear and uncertainty.

Weapons, dress and equipment

Apprehensive at the prospect of combat, the legionary practises thrusting his *spatha* (**1**) with his right hand. In his left hand he grips a curved rectangular *scutum* (shield; **2**) bearing the decoration associated with the *legio XIIII Gemina Martia Victrix*. Although the column of Marcus Aurelius shows all troops carrying curved oval shields, none has been found by archaeologists, and we know that curved rectangular shields remained in use into the 3rd century, the only surviving example coming from Dura Europos and dating from AD 256/57.

He wears a *galea* (helmet; **3**) on his head and *lorica segmentata* (**4**), similar to the near-contemporary Corbridge A finds from Hadrian's Wall, over a red tunic (**5**) and leggings (**6**). He also wears a *balteus* (military belt; **7**) with *pugio* (dagger; **8**) attached and *calcei* (military boots with hobnails; **9**); these became more popular from the 1st century AD onwards, especially in colder climates.

Lucius Verus is depicted in this portrait from the Louvre Museum in Paris, currently at the Metropolitan Museum in New York (L.2007.26). Verus was Marcus Aurelius' adoptive younger brother; Marcus was nine years older. Although he led the campaign in the Parthian Wars and participated actively in the forthcoming Marcomannic Wars, Verus is not given any credit for military activity in the sources. These paint him as the 'bad' wastrel counterpart to his 'good' brother Marcus; but Marcus seems to have had genuine affection for him and a trust in his abilities – at least in the appointment of capable subordinates. (PierreSelim/ Wikimedia/CC0)

These two panels of Marcus on the Arch of Constantine show the emperor addressing the troops (*adlocutio*) and an animal sacrifice (*suovetaurilia*). On the left panel we see three different types of armour – *squamata* (scale), *segmentate* (banded), and a peculiar armour on the left consisting of small square panels each with a central hole – and different *signa*, *aquilae* and *vexilla*. We also see *aquilae*, of which there was only one per legion, and one image of the emperor (the *imago*, carried by the *imaginifer*). The *suovetaurilia* depicted on the right panel involved the sacrifice of a pig (*sus*), a sheep (*ovis*) and a bull (*taurus*), sacrificed to the god Mars to purify the land. (Prisma/UIG/Getty Images)

Dio (55.23.1–24.9) gives an extensive account of the Roman legions, made up of Roman citizens and ostensibly those at the time of Augustus (r. 27 BC–AD 14), although he includes legions created down to his own time. There were 25 legions under Augustus but by Dio's time – the late 2nd or early 3rd century AD – 'only nineteen of them still exist' (55.23.2). Dio goes on to give us (55.23.2–7) details of the legions and their provinces: *II Augusta* (Britannia Superior), *III Gallica* (Phoenicia), *III Cyrenaica* (Arabia), *III Augusta* (Numidia), *IV Scythia* (Syria), *V Macedonica* (Dacia), *VI Victrix* (Britannia Inferior), *VI Ferrata* (Judaea), *VII Claudia* (Moesia Superior), *VIII Augusta* (Germania Superior), *X Gemina* (Pannonia Superior), *X Fretensis* (Judaea), *XI Claudia* (Moesia Inferior), *XII Fulminata* (Cappadocia), *XIII Gemina* (Dacia), *XIIII Gemina Martia Victrix* (Pannonia Superior), *XV Apollinaris* (Cappadocia), *XX Valeria Victrix* (Britannia Superior) and *XXII Primigenia* (Germania Superior). Dio has made some errors here: the *legio XXII Deiotariana* was taken over by Augustus but disbanded in 136, whereas the *legio XXII Primigenia* was founded by Caligula (r. AD 37–41) in AD 39. Other new legions had been formed in the interim (55.24.2–4): Nero (r. AD 54–68) raised *I Italica* (Moesia Inferior); Galba (r. AD 68–69) raised *I Adiutrix* (Pannonia Inferior) and *VII Gemina* (Hispania); Vespasian (r. AD 69–79) raised *II Adiutrix* (Pannonia Inferior), *IIII Flavia* (Moesia Superior) and *XVI Flavia* (Syria); Domitian (r. AD 81–96) raised *I Minervia* (Germania Inferior); Trajan (r. AD 98–117) raised *II Aegyptia* and *XXX Germanica*; and Marcus Aurelius raised *II Italica* (Noricum) and *III Italica* (Raetia). An inscription in Rome (*ILS* 2288) tells us of 28 legions during Marcus' reign and, with his two newly created ones, there were 30 legions across the empire. Dio goes beyond these to mention (55.24.3–4) *I Parthica* and *III Parthica*, founded by Septimius Severus (r. AD 193–211) and stationed in Mesopotamia and Italy respectively; he tells us that these were all the legions then current, however, and – save for the last two – available to Marcus during his reign. Many of these legions had vast institutional experience of wars throughout the empire and had served on many fronts although, as noted, much of this

A close-up of one of the captive chieftain panels on the Arch of Constantine. These panels were repurposed for Constantine's Arch in the 4th century and had the head of the emperor replaced. Note the different Roman armour and helmets – somewhat problematically, there is a ring-helmet depicted here, just as can be seen on the Column of Marcus Aurelius. Note the Roman leggings (worn by legionaries in colder northern climes) of differing lengths – those worn by the figure in the centre end above his knee whereas the others come below the knee. There are also three different intricate shield designs shown. Note, too that, as was the fashion in the reign of Marcus Aurelius, even the legionaries are bearded. (Prisma/UIG/Getty Images)

experience had been depleted through the effects of the plague. We know vexillations (detachments) from various legions were detached to fight in various campaigns. This expedient may have been a deliberate development in the deployment of Roman forces to meet individual challenges (MacDowall 2013: 12), or it may have reflected the crisis of manpower faced by Rome in the wake of the plague.

Combined with the details of the manpower shortage faced by Marcus, Cassius Dio and *ILS* 2288 give us a reasonable idea of the numbers of men available to Rome and the struggles facing them in the Marcomannic Wars.

ORGANIZATION AND COMMAND

Barbarian

Tacitus describes (*Germania* 38) the Marcomanni and Quadi as sub-tribes of the Suebi (or Suevi) people, the most populous of Germania, even though they were not a single tribe. In this, however, we can see that the Suebian knot, which is depicted on several monuments of the Marcomannic Wars, was something we should expect in a sub-division of those people – Tacitus also tells us that other tribes imitated it.

Tacitus relates (*Germania* 42) that both the Marcomanni and Quadi were ruled by kings. Even though we are given names for only some of those rulers, this state of affairs would still seem to have been the case in the 160s and 170s. Tacitus also tells us that 'the strength and power of the monarch depend on Roman influence' (*Germania* 42). In terms of the acceptance or not of a king by a Roman emperor, this would also seem to have been the case during Marcus' reign, although, obviously, the Germanic kings during his reign sought to assert their independence from Rome. We have Ballomar named as king of the Marcomanni and Furtius as a king of the Quadi, and are told of Marcus' refusal to accept Furtius' replacement, Ariogaesus. An inscription also names Valao as chief of the Naristi, allies of the Marcomanni. Tacitus asserts, too, that the Germanic king 'is occasionally supported by our arms, more frequently by our money, and his authority is none the less'(*Germania* 42). Given that we are told of some tribes offering to be Roman allies against the various peoples fighting against the empire during the Marcomannic Wars, this too would seem to have remained the situation.

Under the kings would have been lesser chieftains, each with a number of warriors; how these men were organized is unknown. When Germanic troops were recruited into the auxiliary forces of the Roman Army – whether as infantry cohorts (*cohortes peditatae*, sing. *cohors peditata*), cavalry wings (*alae*, sing. *ala*) or mixed cohorts of cavalry and infantry (*cohortes equitatae*, sing. *cohors equitata*) – they were designated *quingenaria*, indicating a strength of

about 500 infantry (infantry cohorts) or 500 infantry and 120 cavalry (mixed cohorts). There were also double-strength units (*cohortes peditatae miliariae* and *cohortes equitatae miliariae*), which had 800–1,000 men each. Such auxiliary units may have maintained their own distinct fighting style, and we do not know whether the numbers reflected their usual tribal organization. There was also a strict ranking of these units (in Roman eyes): the cavalry wings were the most prestigious, followed by the infantry cohorts and the mixed cohorts.

Tacitus tells us (*Germania* 27) that up to that point he has given the characteristics of the Germanic people as a whole. From that point on he concentrates on specific peoples. Nevertheless, some of Tacitus' descriptions of other tribes are both relevant and likely to be accurate when describing the Marcomanni and Quadi. Discussing the Chatti, he tells us that they promote their picked men to power and, once promoted, such men were obeyed:

> they keep their ranks, note their opportunities, check their impulses, portion out the day, intrench themselves by night, regard fortune as a doubtful, valour as an unfailing, resource; and what is most unusual, and only given to systematic discipline, they rely more on the general than on the army. Their whole strength is in their infantry, which, in addition to its arms, is laden with iron tools and provisions. (*Germania* 30)

A view of one side panel of the Portonaccio Sarcophagus, showing barbarian prisoners being led across a boat-bridge over a river (the Danube?) and on to captivity in Rome. This matches the description in Dio and suggests a setting of the campaign in 172 or after. Again, we have oval shields for the Roman troops, although there is a variety of equipment depicted (including ring-helmets on the front and opposite side panels). Several of the helmets seem highly and individually decorated (one with a ram; the next with a bear). (Mondadori Portfolio/ Getty Images)

The other side panel on the Portonaccio Sarcophagus shows barbarian chieftains submitting to an unarmoured Roman official. Various Roman equipment is shown (more ring-helmets) and the barbarians' hexagonal shields. There is a mixture of Roman armour shown: *segmentata* is worn by the bottom-centre figure of the main scene and *squamata* by the soldiers behind. (DeAgostini/Getty Images)

Although Tacitus states that these attributes characterize the Chatti more than other tribes, we can see that some of these traits are likely to fit what we know of the Marcomanni and Quadi during the wars against Marcus Aurelius. They too seem to have obeyed their commanders and to have displayed some evidence of both discipline and strategy, rather than relying on impetuous charges only.

Roman

The legions of the 2nd century AD were still recruited from Roman citizens; recruits were mostly volunteers although, as we have seen, during the crisis of the 160s this was insufficient and other measures were employed. The organization of the imperial legion remained relatively fixed in the first two centuries AD. The smallest unit was the eight-man tent-section (*contubernium*); each barrack-block in Roman camps would also house a number of *contubernia*. Ten of these made up an 80-man century (*centuria*), which was the legion's smallest tactical subdivision. Six centuries (480 men) made up a cohort and each legion consisted of ten such cohorts. Both Pseudo-Hyginus (3–4) and Vegetius (2.6–8) tell us that the first cohort of each legion consisted of five double-strength centuries, with 800 men. This double strength is confirmed in inscriptions (*CIL* 8.18072) and archaeological remains although Hyginus, writing in the age of Hadrian (r. AD 117–38), gives it a strength of 960 men (*Liber de munitionibus castrorum* 3.1). Thus, the legion consisted of between 5,120 men and the 5,280 of Hyginus (1–5, 42.4); his 5,280 is the number most commonly found. In addition, there were 120 riders attached to each legion, who acted as scouts and dispatch riders (Josephus, *Jewish War* 3.6.2). Thus, the strength of the legion, at least on paper, was 5,400 men. In reality, as the wooden tablets discovered at Vindolanda (Northumberland, England) and dated to slightly earlier in the 2nd century AD have made clear, often the available manpower of a legion may have been significantly less – some men being away on other duties, secondment, sick or on leave. For the campaigns of Marcus, however, we might assume that he did his utmost to bring the legions up to strength. By the time of Alexander Severus (r. AD 222–38) the legion was only 5,000 men according to the (relatively untrustworthy) *SHA* (*Severus Alexander* 50.5), although it later rises to 6,000 (Vegetius, 1.17).

Dio's description goes on (55.24.5–8) to enumerate that there were other troops available to Marcus: the four urban cohorts (*cohortes urbanae*; 2,000

In total there are eight Marcus Aurelius panels reused on the Arch of Constantine. The first two panels from the north face of the arch show the arrival (*adventus*) of the emperor in Rome and the gods' greeting. We can see Mars (shown as a hoplite with Corinthian helmet, muscled cuirass and *pteruges*). The right-hand panel shows Marcus' departure (*profectio*) from the city, the emperor greeted by a personification of the Via Flaminia, the road leading north. (dcastor/Wikimedia/CC0)

men) and the nine cohorts of the Praetorian Guard (4,500 men, almost the size of a legion). The Praetorian Guard accompanied Marcus as it had accompanied Lucius Verus in the Parthian War; two of its commanders fell during the Marcomannic Wars. In addition to these were the 'allied forces of infantry, cavalry and sailors whatever their numbers may have been (for I cannot state the exact figures)' (Dio, 55.24.5). This lack of detail for the auxiliaries is standard in our written sources (with the exception of Arrian's *Ektaxis kat' Alanon*; the Latin title *Acies contra Alanos* has also often been used) and we must rely on inscriptions to estimate the vast number of auxiliary troops used in concert with the legions – numbers usually considered equal to the number of legionaries present on campaign. According to Dio (55.24.6), the bodyguards were 10,000 in number, organized into ten (double-strength) cohorts; the city watch (*Vigiles*) numbered 6,000 men in four divisions.

These last two descriptions seem to involve slight errors – the 10,000 bodyguards may describe the Praetorian Guard, which doubled in size under Septimius Severus, and the *Vigiles* were 7,000 strong in seven 1,000-man cohorts (see Webster 1998: 97–101). The cavalry bodyguard is not mentioned; the cavalry arm of the imperial bodyguard (*equites singulares Augusti*) was a double-strength wing (1,000 men strong) that accompanied the emperor on campaign, although it was 2,000 men by Severus' reign. Dio does, though, mention the Batavians, picked allied German cavalrymen who acted as an additional bodyguard (the *custodes*), although he states: 'I cannot, however, give their exact number any more than I can that of the Evocati' (55.24.8). The *evocati* were veterans who had retired but re-enlisted as a vexillation for a particular campaign.

Command of imperial legions deferred to the emperor in two ways. Technically, it was the emperor who commanded the entire army through his *imperium maius* (supreme command). As overall commander he would appoint men to command imperial provinces and legions in his stead. Many of the appointments were made through the emperor's goodwill and he appointed subordinates as commanders of whole provinces and of legions.

Each legion was commanded by a *legatus legionis*, usually a senator who had already been a *praetor* or a *quaestor* (the initial posts in a senatorial career) and had military experience. During the Marcomannic Wars we find several men who commanded more than one legion in succession. Equestrians too could command legions: usually after command of auxiliary units they would be adlected to the senate and, although older than senatorial candidates, they too would hold quaestorships and praetorships after which they could be appointed *legati*. The emperor could also choose to promote a candidate to an extraordinary post such as the command of more than one province.

Prior to holding the first magistracy on an imperial career, the quaestorship, usually at around the age of 25, a Roman commander would have held one of the tribuneships in the legion. Each legion had six tribuneships, the most senior being the *tribunus laticlavius* ('broad-stripe tribune'), a senatorial position; the remaining five were *tribuni angusticlavii* (sing. *tribunus angusticlavius*, 'narrow-stripe tribune'), made up of men of equestrian rank. The senatorial candidate would then hold the quaestorship and take up an administrative position within a province before holding the praetorship and advancing to the command of a legion. An equestrian candidate could become the prefect

of an auxiliary cohort and then a *tribunus angusticlavius* before moving on to be the *praefectus* (prefect) of an auxiliary cavalry wing, a *praefectus alae*. He might then become a procurator of a province or, for the select few, gain senatorial rank (at the emperor's prerogative) and begin a senatorial career, albeit at a greater age (but often with much more experience).

After holding a position (or positions) as *legatus legionis*, a senator would hope to hold the consulship and go on to be the governor of an imperial province, especially one with a military force, a *legatus Augusti pro praetore*, a 'legate of the emperor with authority of a praetor'. Under his direct command would be the commander(s) of any legions in his province. There were also senatorial provinces, the appointment to which was approved by the senate (and named proconsul), although these usually had a minimal military force at the governor's disposal and were not normally on the frontiers. Often the sources do not include these precise terms or they use an abbreviation of them. In both the literary and epigraphic evidence for the Marcomannic Wars, we find all manner of commanders named, often with their careers recorded in minute detail.

In the lower ranks of the Roman Army, its backbone was provided by each legion's 60 centurions, usually career soldiers with vast experience, each commanding 80 men. The centurionate had a strict hierarchical order. These men could hope to rise to become the *primus pilus*, the chief centurion of a legion who commanded the first century of the first cohort. Other positions

The second set of two Marcus Aurelius panels on the north face of the Arch of Constantine. Here we see an act of largess to the people (*largitio*). This panel shows clearly that Commodus has been removed, probably during the *damnatio memoriae* ('condemnation of memory' – where a figure and their name are removed from monuments and inscriptions and derided in literature) of that emperor after his death in 193. It is more likely it was removed then rather than later when the panel was reused as part of the Arch of Constantine. The panel on the right shows a Germanic chieftain being brought before Marcus, included to show clemency (*clementia*). We see two standard-bearers (*signiferi*) with animal-skin headdress and, behind, three legionary standards (*signa*), and an eagle standard (*aquila*) with a *vexillum*. (dcastor/Wikimedia/CC0)

Dating from 142, the right-hand panel of the Bridgeness Slab from Bo'ness on the Antonine Wall in Scotland shows both a *vexillum* (with the name of the legion inscribed) and a *suovetaurilia*. The purification of Rome and other places is a theme of the surviving literature around the Marcomannic Wars and it is clear that Marcus Aurelius went to great lengths – such as inviting and welcoming the participation of other religious groups – to ensure that such purification took place. On the left, a Roman cavalryman runs down naked Pictish enemies. The fact that the Picts are shown with typical small square shields supports the idea that other reliefs do offer useful details of equipment. (Barnimg/Wikimedia/CC BY-SA 3.0)

included the camp prefect (*praefectus castrorum*), usually an equestrian officer, who was third in command after the *legatus* and *tribunus laticlavius*. The pinnacle of this professional career was to become the *praefectus* of the Praetorian Guard. The men of the legion too had a series of promotions they could gain to be better paid and take on additional duties with the hope of one day being promoted to the centurionate, candidates for which were usually approved by the provincial governor.

In addition to these appointments, the emperor also had a council of advisers (*consilium principis*) present with him on campaign. Other commanders, and the replacements for those who fell, were chosen by Marcus and his advisers even though there was a clear pathway and *cursus honorum* ('course of honours', the typical progression or ladder for a political career) for men to be eligible for military commands from both the senatorial and equestrian ranks. The careers of men such as Valerius Maximianus show the equestrian path perfectly, as do other inscriptions – such as *ILS* 1107 and *CIL* 6.1449, concerning Marcus Vindex (the son of the prefect), which tells us he was a governor of Moesia Inferior and Moesia Superior. Prior to that he had been procurator in Dacia Malvensis, prefect of the *ala III Thracum* and then the *ala I Ulpia contariorum*, prefect of the *cohors VI Gallorum*, in which post he was decorated by Marcus during the Germanic wars with two untipped spears, two standards and a mural and rampart crown. The inscription, put up by his wife and daughter, tells us he lived 42 years and five months.

TACTICS AND EQUIPMENT

Barbarian

Tacitus states (*Germania* 13) that the wearing of arms in Germanic culture was only for those who had been recognized as a man. It is possible that a rite of passage was when a youth was equipped 'with a shield and spear' (*Germania* 13); Tacitus tells his readers that these arms were to the tribesman what the toga was to the young Roman who was first presented with his *toga virilis* ('toga of manhood' usually adopted between the ages of 14 and 18). We also see many swords, usually longer *spathae*, although on some depictions it is clear that any sword could be shown. Elsewhere in the *Germania*, Tacitus discusses the German tribes and Sarmatians at the same time despite telling us that the Sarmatians use cavalry whereas the Germanic tribes of the Venetii carry shields and value 'strength and fleetness of foot' (*Germania* 46). The Marcomanni are described as standing 'first in strength and renown, and their very territory, from which the Boii were driven in a former age, was won by valour. Nor are the Narisci and Quadi inferior to them' (*Germania* 42). From this we might surmise that the two tribes might be equal in numbers. Peculiarly, the Naristi appear only once in the literary accounts of Marcus' wars (Dio, 71/72.21), but they are also mentioned on the inscription to Valerius Maximianus (*AE* 1956.124) as being defeated. According to Dio, they provided only 3,000 settlers, presumably a count including only the men who would be recruited into the Roman Army and so representing, perhaps, a decline in that tribe's strength. In his section on Germanic peoples in general, Tacitus describes their mode of dress:

> They all wrap themselves in a cloak which is fastened with a clasp, or, if this is not forthcoming, with a thorn, leaving the rest of their persons bare. They pass whole days on the hearth by the fire. The wealthiest are distinguished by a dress which is not flowing, like that of the Sarmatians and Parthians, but is tight, and exhibits each limb. They also wear the skins of wild beasts; the tribes on the Rhine and Danube in a careless fashion, those of the interior with more elegance, as not obtaining other clothing by commerce. These select certain animals, the hides of which they strip off and vary them with the spotted skins of beasts, the produce of the outer ocean, and of seas unknown to us. The women have the same dress as the men, except that they generally wrap themselves in linen garments, which they embroider with purple, and do not lengthen out the upper part of their clothing into sleeves. The upper and lower arm is thus bare, and the nearest part of the bosom is also exposed. (*Germania* 17)

Some of this is borne out in how tribesmen are shown in relief and sculpture – trousers, tunics and cloaks especially – and also in surviving archaeological

The well-preserved remains of the mail found at Vimose on the island of Funen, Denmark. Although iron was not well preserved at the Thorsberg site, there were some fragments of mail. Other sites with contemporary deposits such as Nydam Bog (near Sønderborg, Denmark), Illerup Ådal (near Skanderborg in East Jutland, Denmark) and Vimose have preserved swords and other weapons, shield bosses and armour. A padding garment would have been worn under the mail, but the only example preserved from antiquity comes from Dura Europos in the 3rd century. (Martijn Wijnhoven)

A Germanic spearhead from Vimose in Denmark, early 3rd century AD. A variety of spearheads have survived in various burial and deposit finds; often the shaft has completely deteriorated. This leaf-shaped example is common, but many are barbed, perhaps made as hunting spears (although they could also have been used in combat). The spear was the weapon by which a Germanic youth was identified as a man, in addition to his shield. (Odense Bys Museer/Wikimedia/CC BY-SA 2.0)

finds. Tacitus tells us that common practices among the Chatti were 'letting the hair and beard grow as soon as they have attained manhood' (*Germania* 31) and proving their prowess in battle by killing an enemy. Nearly all depictions of the enemy across all the media relating to the Marcomannic Wars include bearded tribesmen, which might imply that this practice was widespread. Tacitus tells us here too that cowards and the unwarlike remain unshorn. This, too, might be part of the Roman presentation of the Marcomannic Wars – all their opponents were warlike and veteran warriors. Tacitus adds (*Germania* 31) that the bravest of them also wore a torque and we see this in some depictions too. Such men began the battle and made up the first line. Although this account is given in reference to the Chatti, it might relate to other tribes as well.

Beyond seeking to surround the Romans on various occasions and relying on the impetus of their charge, our sources do not provide any evidence of subtlety in Germanic tactics. They raided and plundered in great numbers and tried to return across the Danube without being caught. Several of the Germanic forces' victories seem to have come about because they outnumbered the smaller Roman forces arrayed against them. At the same time, however, we can discern more strategic and even tactical thinking. For example, the invasion of 170 saw the tribesmen target Aquileia and Opitergium; this was surely deliberate and the result of a far more complex strategic idea than simple plunder, requiring as it did the abilities and technologies necessary to conduct a siege. More than that, the invaders seem to have timed their disruptions to coincide with moments when Rome was weak or distracted. They also seem to have deliberately captured vast numbers of prisoners in 170 to be returned for payments they knew would come. What is more, the name 'Battle on the Ice' implies that the Iazyges and their allies lured the Romans on to the ice to fight a battle on their terms. Germanic tactics do,

Germanic shields dating from the 3rd century AD, preserved in the Thorsberg Moor bog. Although the wood (unusually) is in excellent condition, any decoration has not survived. (Einsamer Schütze/Wikimedia/CC BY-SA 3.0)

however, seem to have relied upon charges, either of infantry or of cavalry and infantry combined, in which the warriors could display their valour to their chiefs. In some cases during the Marcomannic Wars, such as at Carnuntum, these tactics were successful; in others, especially where the Romans were able to weather the initial enemy charge, the emperor's men could prevail by harnessing their superior discipline and tactics.

Roman

Most of our descriptions of battles during the Principate are unsatisfactory in terms of exactly how Roman armies were deployed. In the analysis of the Battle on the Ice below, I make an argument that we may be able to use Arrian's *Ektaxis kat' Alanon*, which gives us a detailed deployment of both legionaries and auxiliary troops. Although I argue that we may be able to use it to cast light on a battle against the Sarmatian Iazyges and their Quadi allies, however, it is usually considered to be a unique deployment and not one transferable to other battles.

Only one source describes how a legion was usually deployed. Vegetius, writing in the 4th century AD but compiling his *Epitoma rei militaris* from a combination of earlier sources, tells us (2.6) that, in the front line, the first cohort of the legion was deployed first on the right, then the second, the third in the centre, then the fourth, and the fifth on the left. Behind the first five cohorts in a second line were the sixth on the right behind the first cohort, then the seventh, the eighth in the centre of the second line, then the ninth, and the tenth cohort on the left of the second line behind the fifth cohort. In the absence of other information, we can use this evidence when considering how legions were deployed, although for the Marcomannic Wars it is not always clear how many legions fought in a given action. Sometimes only one legion is singled out, even when it is clear there were more men involved on the Roman side, such as at Carnuntum in 170 and the Miracle of the Rain in 174, where the *legio XIIII Gemina Martia Victrix* and *legio XII Fulminata* are highlighted respectively. There were probably vexillations from other legions, but they are (usually) unnamed.

On multiple occasions in the Marcomannic Wars we are told that the Romans withstood the enemy charges by forming into compact order. The *testudo* (tortoise) formation is not described on those occasions – although it is shown in a single scene on the Column of Marcus Aurelius – but this was probably a locked-shield formation with which the Romans weathered the storm of the enemy charge.

Gladius blades of the Mainz type. The term *gladius* ('sword') was used for all manner of blades, as opposed to Greek terms like *xiphos, kopis, machaira* and the earlier Latin word *ensis*. Originally, however, it was used to designate the *gladius Hispaniensis* in the 3rd century BC, a sword useful for both thrusting and slashing if necessary. This became the Roman sword of the legions for centuries thereafter. There were several types of *gladius* in the first two centuries AD with only subtle differences between them – hence the Pompeii, Fulham and Mainz *gladius* types, named after find spots. The Pompeii type seems to have been the most popular. By the 3rd century AD, most *gladii* had been replaced by *spathae*, longer swords that were initially used only by cavalry but were adopted by infantry forces. This process had probably begun earlier in the 2nd century and was widespread by the time of the Marcomannic and Sarmatian wars. The blades of *gladii* had been getting longer, from 40cm up to 55cm, so this was an understandable progression. Two contemporary *spatha* blades from Canterbury in England had blades of 85cm and 90cm. (MatthiasKabel/ Wikimedia/CC BY 2.5)

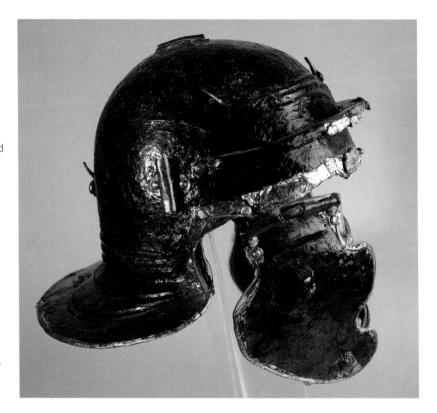

A Mainz-Weisenau-type helmet from Bescançon, France. Some of its tinning decoration is preserved along with other decorations. Although several helmet types were being worn in the same period by Roman soldiers, the depictions in Roman art show only a limited number, and often no find has matched those depicted in art. The range of helmets worn in the mid- to late-2nd century AD covers the types classified by Henry Russell Robinson (1975) as Imperial Italic D, E, G and H (of which the Niedermörmter helmet is the best preserved example), and Imperial Gallic H and I, perhaps even G (the Mainz-Weisenau type), although it is usually dated to the 1st century AD and only early in the 2nd. (DEA/G. DAGLI ORTI/Getty Images)

Each legionary was protected by his armour and shield, much more so than his opponents. Each legionary was armed with a throwing javelin – either a *pilum* (pl. *pila*) or some other sort: the terms *verutum*, *lancea* and *spiculum* are also used in the sources. Most artistic depictions, however, both the Column of Marcus Aurelius and several funerary sculptures, show legionaries of the age using thrusting spears (*hastae*, sing. *hasta*). It may be that missile troops were provided by the several auxiliary units listed in inscriptions though often missing from literary sources. Javelins are shown in use during hand-to-hand combat, but the legionary also had his *spatha* or *gladius*.

This 'lump' of Roman mail armour, *lorica hamata*, is now on display at the Aalen Limes Museum, Baden-Württemberg, Germany, the site of Kastell Buch, the largest Roman cavalry fort north of the Alps and situated in the Roman province of Raetia. Very few examples of Roman mail survive, so our best clues are to be found in the depiction of such armour on sculpture and relief. (Wolfgang Sauber/ Wikimedia/CC BY-SA 4.0)

Carnuntum

AD 170

BACKGROUND TO BATTLE

In the *SHA* (*Marcus* 12–15), we get a very brief account of the entire Marcomannic Wars. A similar summary is offered in the epitome of Dio's books 71 and 72. The *SHA* tells us that while Lucius Verus was engaged in the Parthian War, the Marcomannic Wars broke out 'after having been postponed for a long time by the diplomacy of the men who were in charge there, in order that the Marcomannic war might not be waged until Rome was done with the war in the East' (*Marcus* 12.13). When Verus returned to Rome, Marcus advised the senate that both men would be needed to conduct the German war. The situation did not change when Verus' returning army brought plague back to the imperial capital. This, the Antonine Plague or Plague of Galen, was one of the most devastating epidemics of the ancient world; it may have claimed the lives of up to 10 per cent of the population. Marcus needed to purify the city (a lustration) and so summoned 'priests from all sides, performed foreign religious ceremonies, and purified the city in every way' (*SHA, Marcus* 13.1).

In Dio we get the summary that the 'emperor himself fought for a long time, almost his entire life, one might say, with the barbarians in the region of the Ister, with both the Iazyges and the Marcomanni, one after the other, using Pannonia as his base' (71/72.3). The summary does, fortunately, go on to give us more detail, although it is abundantly clear that much has been lost. In Herodian (1.2.5), we find an even briefer summary noting that many other capable authors had already recorded the political and military enterprises Marcus had undertaken against the barbarians in the north and the east. Unfortunately, the works of those other authors have not survived.

Dio goes on to give a somewhat garbled account (71/72.3.1), telling us that 6,000 Langobardi and Obii crossed the Ister River, but were defeated by cavalry under Marcus Vindex – the *ala Ulpia Cantariorum*, according to Elliott (2020: 103) – and infantry – vexillations from the *legio I Adiutrix* – commanded by Candidus. The barbarians were completely routed and they sent envoys to Marcus Iallius Bassus, the governor of Pannonia, to negotiate peace. As their leader, the barbarians chose Ballomar, king of the Marcomanni, and ten others, one for each nation: 'These envoys made peace, which they ratified with oaths, and then returned home' (Dio, 71/72.3.1). The very next sentence states: 'Many of the Germans, too, from across the Rhine, advanced as far as Italy' (Dio, 71/72.3.2). The invasions defeated by Vindex and Candidus probably occurred in 166 (Elliott 2020: 103) or 167 (Birley 1987: 161), however, whereas the invaders reached Italy only in 170 (and after the battle of Carnuntum).

The *SHA* returns to its account of the war: 'Clad in the military cloak the two emperors finally set forth, for now not only were the Victuali and Marcomanni throwing everything into confusion, but other tribes, who had been driven on by the more distant barbarians and had retreated before them, were ready to attack Italy if not peaceably received' (*Marcus* 14.1). When the emperors reached Aquileia, they learned that several of the kings had retreated (at their approach?) together with their peoples and had put the agitators to death. The kings also asked pardon of the emperors. The Quadi, who had lost their king, assured the Romans that they would not appoint a successor unless he was approved by the Roman emperors (*SHA, Marcus* 14.3). Detail of actions is slight indeed. The *SHA* tells us that Verus thought the expedition could return to Rome 'because Furius Victorinus, the prefect of the guard, had been lost, and part of his army had perished' (*Marcus* 14.5). This may not have been due to fighting but to the effects of the plague, hence Verus' desire to return to Rome. We get no more detail of the campaign in Verus' absence, and we must turn elsewhere for it.

Marcus, however, considered that the expedition should continue on its way, 'thinking that the barbarians, in order that they might not be crushed by the size of so great a force, were feigning a retreat and using other ruses which afford safety in war, held that they should persist in order that they might not be overwhelmed by the mere burden of their vast preparations' (*SHA, Marcus* 14.5). The brother-emperors crossed the Alps and 'completed all measures necessary for the defence of Italy and Illyricum' (*SHA, Marcus* 14.6), Illyricum being the old name for the Pannonian provinces (Birley 1987: 157). They toured the provinces and reached Carnuntum (*AE* 1982.777) and set up the *praetentura Italiae et Alpium*, a new command of the Italian and Alpine front under the command of Quintus Antistius Adventus. He was given command of the two newly raised legions, the *legio II Pia* and the *legio III Concordia*. The emperors spent the winter of 168/69 at Aquileia, but it was decided in January or February 169 that Verus should return to Rome to attend to the pressing matter of plague management in the capital. This seems to have been at Verus' insistence and both emperors set out on the return journey. On the way, however, 'Lucius died from a stroke of apoplexy while riding in the carriage with his brother' (*SHA, Marcus* 14.7). He was 38 years old.

Verus' death, possibly a result of the plague his own army brought back from the East, caused yet further delays to the execution of the war in the north. Marcus accompanied the body back to Rome, where Verus was deified, and Marcus Aurelius was now left to rule the empire alone. In many ways, a man preoccupied with Stoic philosophy was ill-suited to waging war, and yet the Roman military system was such that there was no shortage of military leaders to wage war competently on their emperor's

A statue of the personification of the Danube, the god Danubius. For those living close to the river, especially as it was such an important conduit for the life of the fort at Carnuntum, worshipping the river was hardly surprising. There is evidence of all manner of gods worshipped at Carnuntum, including Egyptian deities, the Roman god Mithras, and the supreme god, Jupiter Heliopolitanus. This tallies not only with the polyglot nature of the legion and the life of a Roman legionary fort, but also with the number of gods Marcus enlisted before the campaigns in 170 to purify the Roman Army. (Jona Lendering/CC0 1.0 Universal)

behalf. Our surviving sources seldom mention commanders, however, and we rely on the ample epigraphic and archaeological evidence of men who commanded for Marcus but whose names are not recorded in the literary record – men such as Marcus Valerius Maximianus and perhaps Marcus Vindex (son of the man named in the sources). Maximianus' remarkable career is recorded in two inscriptions: at Laugaricio (modern-day Trenčin, Slovakia: *CIL* 3.13439) in 179 and another at Diana Veteranorum (modern-day Ain Zana, Algeria: *AE* 1956.124).

In late 169, the plague was still raging in Rome. The return of the legions from the Parthian War (and those men returning to the widespread bases from which they had been seconded) meant it spread quickly. The *SHA* (*Marcus* 21.6–8) and other sources tell us that there was a manpower shortage, which the emperor sought to address by forming the two new legions –*II Pia* and *III Concordia*, later renamed *II Italica* and *III Italica* – as well as recruiting slaves, gladiators and even bandits. Marcus even fielded units of Germanic auxiliaries against Germanic enemies, in contravention of the usual practice of avoiding making men fight those with whom they might have an affinity. The *SHA* and other sources (Eutropius, *Breviarium* 8.12; Orosius, *History* 7.15.5–6) suggest the severity of the crisis facing Marcus. Rather than raise taxes, Marcus sold off imperial furniture to fund several of these recruitment reforms and fund the war effort, aware that a new tax would have been immensely unpopular – and, given the circumstances of the people, probably fruitless (*SHA*, *Marcus* 17.4–5, 21.9). From this point, however, the brief summary in the *SHA* ceases to be of use to us as it glosses over much and simply records that the emperor 'overwhelmed the Marcomanni while they were crossing the Danube' (*Marcus* 21.10). This is probably a reference to actions in 172, so gets us too far ahead of our narrative.

At some point in 169, the governor of Dacia, Calpurnius Agricola, died – we do not know if he died of the plague or in battle. The governor of neighbouring Moesia Superior, Claudius Fronto, took over part of Dacia; later that year or in 170, Fronto took over command of the whole province.

Although the emperor probably wanted to return to the front quickly, in late summer 170, probably September, Marcus' seven-year-old son Annius Verus died after a surgery to remove a tumour. The emperor grieved for only five days before heading to the north.

MAP KEY

1 The Marcomanni, Quadi and other allies cross the Danube *en masse*. One invading contingent makes its way towards Aquileia and Opitergium, 500km to the south-west, through Pannonia Superior and Dalmatia; others ravage Pannonia Superior.

2 The Roman garrison at Carnuntum, including the *legio XIIII Gemina Martia Victrix* based at the fort and reinforced with additional troops, marches out to intercept the ravaging invaders. Some distance from Carnuntum, the Roman force is surrounded by the overwhelming numbers of the Marcomanni, Quadi and their allies. The Roman force is defeated and 20,000 men are lost.

3 The Marcomanni, Quadi and other allies put Aquileia under siege.

4 Opitergium is plundered by the invaders before any Roman response from Moesia can be made.

5 The Roman response, coming from Sirmium or Singidunum, eventually catches up with the invaders who are, by this time, on their way back to the Danube.

Battlefield environment

Of the three battles examined in this volume, the battle of Carnuntum is the one with the clearest definition of a site (although 'Carnuntum' was not the contemporary name for the battle). Beyond the name of the legionary fortress that was the most likely base for troops in the area, however, we have little to work with. It would seem that the battle was not a siege involving the fort, despite the concurrent operations against Opitergium and Aquileia involving siege warfare.

The best solution seems to be that the Roman garrison and additional troops moved out of the fort to try to check the incursion of the Marcomanni and their allies. They were then surrounded and defeated. If this was the case,

then the tribes may have crossed the Danube upstream or downstream from the site of Carnuntum, but close enough for it to provide the name of the battle.

It is not clear how the invaders crossed the river. In Lucian's account, the Romans' defeat followed the botched sacrifice of two lions when the river was swimmable. This might suggest a width of the river which was not too extreme; but although we are told that the defeat followed on soon after this sacrifice, it is not made clear exactly where the battle occurred, or how the tribesmen crossed *en masse*, although the battle may have been fought close to the river.

A model of Sirmium at Sremska Mitrovika, Serbia, located in Pannonia Inferior on the Save (or Sava) River. Pannonia Superior had Carnuntum as its capital and Pannonia Inferior had two capitals, one at Sirmium, the other at Aquincum. Sirmium may have been Marcus' headquarters in 170, especially if he expected to campaign in Dacia and, more likely, later when he campaigned against the Iazyges specifically. Singidunum, in Moesia, is a less likely candidate as a headquarters for Marcus, as it lay further away from the river border. (mediaportal. vojvodina.gov.rs/Wikimedia/ CC BY-SA 3.0)

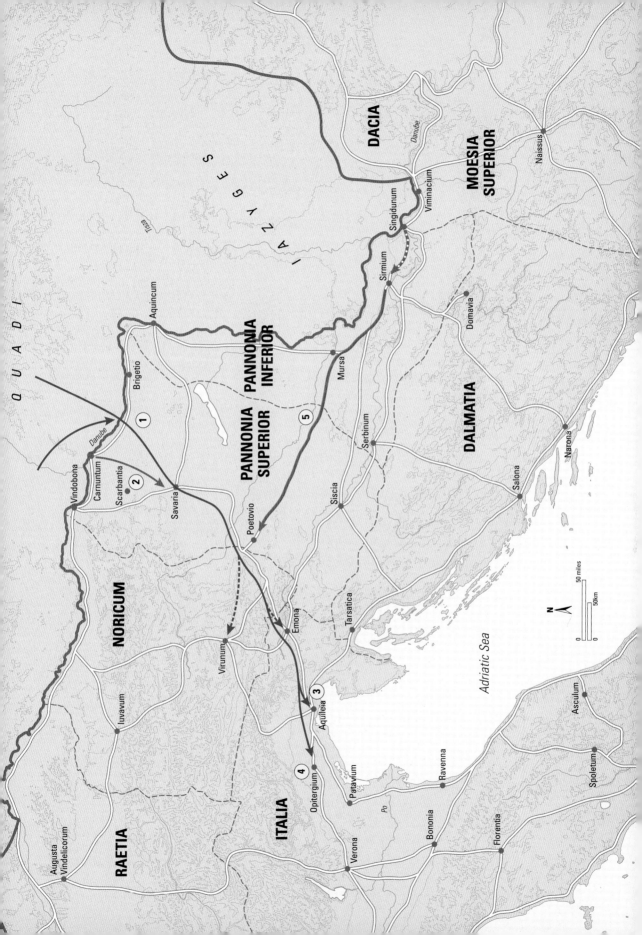

QUADI

DACIA

MOESIA
SUPERIOR

Naissus

Danube

I A Z Y G E S

Tisa

Singidunum

Viminacium

Sirmium

Aquincum

PANNONIA
INFERIOR

Brigetio

①

Domavia

Mursa

Vindobona

Carnuntum

Scarbantia

②

PANNONIA
SUPERIOR

Savaria

⑤

Serbinum

DALMATIA

Narona

Poetovio

Siscia

Salona

Danube

NORICUM

Iuvavum

Tarsatica

Emona

Virunum

Adriatic Sea

③

Aquileia

Asculum

④

Opitergium

Patavium

ITALIA

Ravenna

Spoletum

Po

Verona

Bononia

Florentia

N

50 miles

50km

A bronze coin of Antoninus Pius (r. AD 138–61). Minted in Abonoteichus, it shows the snake god Glycon and the reach of Alexander of Abonoteichus' cult that was so lambasted by Lucian. The snake Alexander operated apparently had a puppet head, the mouth of which he would work by strings. The head wore a blond wig; the hair on the snake is visible in this depiction. The legend has the name Glycon and the name of the city of Abonoteichus (where it was minted): ΓΛΥΚΩΝ ΑΒΩΝΟΤΕΙΧΕΙΤΩΝ ('GLYCON ABONOTEICHEITON'). (CNG/Wikimedia/CC BY-SA 3.0)

INTO COMBAT

As we saw above, the invading force mentioned by Dio (71/72.3.1), numbering only 6,000 Langobardi and Obii, cannot have fought at the battle of Carnuntum; the small size of the force suggests it was one of the earlier raids in 166 or 167 after which peace was made. The measures undertaken by Marcus Aurelius and Lucius Verus in 168 were also intended to restore peace to the frontier. Reportedly, the Marcomanni were one of 11 tribes involved in those earlier raids, but perhaps not the most dominant group, even though their king was chosen as a spokesperson. Ballomar was, presumably, still king of the Marcomanni in 170 when they crossed the Danube in force, again in conjunction with the Quadi, and destroyed the garrison at Carnuntum.

This action was part of a much larger and more serious invasion of Roman territory. Our sources are, however, almost silent on these invasions and we must rely on a very unusual source to corroborate the course of the campaign. The satirist Lucian of Samosata was an exact contemporary and had been present in the East with Verus. He wrote several works during the progress of Verus' campaign and also provides a vast list of the petty historians who attended the court and sought the emperor's favour. Lucian also sought the emperor's favour, but not as a historian; he wrote several entertaining and rhetorical works for Verus in Antioch.

Lucian's unexpected relevance for the Marcomannic Wars is in a scathing attack he made on a false prophet named Alexander of Abonoteichus (modern-day İnebolu, Turkey), also known as Alexander the Paphlagonian. He was the founder of a religious cult dedicated to Glycon, an ancient snake god associated with healing, protection and prophecy. According to Lucian, however, Alexander was an unmitigated fraud and swindler. Nevertheless, the cult became immensely popular, especially in the East. Attached to the cult was an oracle in which Alexander would answer the questions of worshippers. During the plague in Rome in 166, a verse from one of his oracles was used as an amulet of protection on the door posts of believers in the city.

As part of Marcus Aurelius' measures to purify the city and his ongoing measures to ensure the purity of the army, Alexander was summoned to Rome and despatched with the army towards Pannonia. No doubt many in the army had become followers of Alexander while campaigning in the East and now agitated to have the prophet accompany them on the Danube. The *legio XIIII Gemina Martia Victrix* had fought in Lucius Verus' Parthian War and was now based at Carnuntum in Pannonia. Alexander's most powerful supporter was the elderly senator Publius Mummius Sisenna Rutilianus, who had been consul in 146 and reached the pinnacle of prestige for a senatorial career in 160 when he was appointed *proconsul Asiae*; it was usual that a senator would retire after such an appointment. In that office, however, he became a fervent convert to Alexander's teachings (Lucian, *Alexander the False Prophet* 30). In his sixties, Rutilianus even married Alexander's daughter. Lucian tells us that he personally thwarted Alexander's attempt to murder Rutilianus (his wife, Alexander's daughter, would inherit the senator's wealth), but went unrewarded.

Back in Rome, Rutilianus' support of Alexander continued unabated, however, and this gave him access to the imperial court. At the outbreak of the

Marcomannic Wars, just as Marcus was about to engage with the Marcomanni and Quadi, and taking advantage of the fear in Rome that prompted Marcus to enrol the adherents of several religions, Alexander pronounced an oracle:

> To rolling Ister, swollen with Heaven's rain,
> Of Cybelean thralls, those mountain beasts,
> Fling you a pair; therewith all flowers and herbs
> Of savour sweet that Indian air does breed.
> Hence victory, and fame, and lovely peace. (*Alexander the False Prophet* 48)

This oracle stated that, to secure victory, two lions should be flung, alive, into the Danube, together with sacred herbs and spices. Lucian goes on to tell us that these instructions were followed to the letter; the lions, however, swam towards the enemy bank of the river, where they were clubbed to death. The barbarians took them to be some new kind of wolf. Lucian concludes his chapter 48 by relating that the Romans immediately met with a severe defeat, suffering 20,000 men lost in a single engagement; this was followed by what he calls the 'Aquileian incident' in which that city was almost lost.

Lucian's last sentence provides the most detail we get of the defeat and the wider sequence of events during the campaign; conspicuous by their absence are detailed battle accounts in the surviving accounts left to us by historians. Alexander made the excuse that Glycon had foretold a victory, but not which side would be victor; this recalled the oracles from Delphi and Amphiaraus at Oropos made to the Lydian king Croesus in 546 BC (Herodotus 1.53.3) that by going to war a great empire would be destroyed. In Herodotus' account, it was unclear which empire would be brought to an end; the result was that it was Croesus' own. Other oracles had been similarly misinterpreted in the centuries since.

We can justifiably suspect that our other sources have purposely glossed over this severe Roman defeat, apparently entailing as it did the loss of 20,000 men or the equivalent of four full legions, probably the legion and some 15,000 auxiliaries and vexillations, or the equivalent of two legions and an equal number of auxiliaries. With Roman losses at this level, the actual force was probably greater still in numbers.

The 'Aquileian incident' refers to the placing of that city under siege by the Marcomanni and Quadi after their victory at Carnuntum. The defeat there opened the invaders' way into Italy and Aquileia was some 500km from Carnuntum. The invaders also sacked Opitergium. Corroboration of Lucian's account comes from a much later source. The historian Ammianus Marcellinus, writing his *Res Gestae* before 391, mentions the siege when referring to the Quadi:

> the Quadi, who had long been quiet, were suddenly aroused to an outbreak; they are a nation now not greatly to be feared, but were formerly immensely warlike and powerful, as is shown by their swift and sudden swoops in former times, their siege of Aquileia in company with the Marcomanni, the destruction of Opitergium, and many other bloody deeds performed in rapid campaigns; so that when they broke through the Julian Alps, the emperor Marcus Pius, of whom we have previously written, could with difficulty check them. (29.6.1)

Unfortunately, the book to which Ammianus refers, in which he dealt with the wars of Marcus in more detail, is entirely lost. If there were any other communities sacked along the way (which there surely were), the sources do not give any details – although Dean (2013: 32) also adds Emona (modern-day Ljublana, Slovenia) and Virunum (modern-day Klagenfurt, Austria) to the list of towns sacked during this invasion.

The significance of the invasion of Italy conducted by the Quadi and Marcomanni cannot be overestimated. The last time foreign barbarians had invaded Italy itself had been in the late 2nd century BC, when the Cimbri and Teutones had defeated several armies before being vanquished by Caius Marius in 102 and 101 BC. Birley posits (van Ackeren 2012: 224) that the invaders must have outflanked the main Roman forces, which were defeated. Carnuntum lies on the southern bank of the Danube and so the Marcomanni or Quadi may have crossed upstream or downstream – there are many places where a crossing could

A statue base from Carnuntum with *legio XIIII Gemina Martia Victrix* obvious and the symbol of the legion, the capricorn, also in evidence. (Jona Lendering/ CC0 1.0 Universal)

have been effected – thereby catching the garrison off guard. This seems more likely than the tribes marching on Carnuntum itself (Elliott 2020: 108), although the invaders did prove to be capable of besieging cities. It seems more likely that they invaded with the intention of raiding and pillaging the provinces, and even Italy, rather than seeking a direct and immediate confrontation with the garrison. One modern commentator has suggested (Koepfer 2013: 25) that contemporary small Roman camps in Raetia, Pannonia and Noricum probably occupied by vexillations showed the Marcomanni outflanking known Roman garrisons.

If we accept that the invading contingent that moved on Aquileia and Opitergium was different from that prevailing at Carnuntum, the implication is that vast numbers of tribesmen and women – Dio gives us the detail of women in armour (71/72.3.2) – crossed over into Roman territory. No source offers numbers of participants in these later Germanic invasions and we must look to another great invasion – that two centuries later, in 376, when we are told by only one source (Eunapius, *Universal History* F42) that 200,000 Goths of a single tribe (the Theruingi) crossed over into the empire. If that number is taken to provide a hint as to how many men were typically in a tribe (and tribes varied in size, of course), then we get a very rough estimate that when the Marcomanni and Quadi invaded, perhaps up to twice that number crossed into Roman territory. The invading forces of the Huns in the 5th century AD were said to number 500,000 (Jordanes, *Getica* 182). A letter dated to 174 tells us of (a surely fanciful) 970,000 barbarians facing the Roman legions (see the account of the Miracle of the Rain below).

There is much scepticism about these numbers, and we do not have to accept them at face value for the Marcomanni and Quadi. Whatever the number, however, there were enough barbarian tribesmen to outnumber, overwhelm and outflank the various Roman forces intended to oppose them. The idea that some invaders could have split off and made their way to Aquileia and Opitergium, or that that action was a separate force entirely, is easily entertained. The road into Italy from Germania via Pannonia was well known because it was the Amber Route from the Baltic, well traversed since at least Nero's day (Pliny the Elder, *Natural History* 37.45–46). Ammianus' phrase 'bloody deeds performed in rapid campaigns' (29.6.1) implies, perhaps, the presence of barbarian cavalry, although no other source goes into detail and Germanic armies had always included large numbers of infantry, especially lightly armed infantry – men who had been recruited as just such troops into Roman armies in centuries past. If this is indeed the case, we can envisage that large numbers of Marcomanni and Quadi crossed the Danube; the soldiers stationed at Carnuntum would have marched out to drive them back over the river, but were overwhelmed, both in terms of overall numbers and the invaders' superior numbers of lightly armed troops, who could outmanoeuvre the heavily equipped Roman legionaries. This was precisely what happened in 172 at the Battle on the Ice (Dio, 71/72.7). The scenario of Rome's legions being surrounded by superior numbers of more lightly armed enemy troops was one that would recur during the Marcomannic Wars.

There is some other information we can apply to enhance our understanding of the battle. Carnuntum, located in Pannonia Superior, was the base of the *legio XIIII Gemina Martia Victrix*. The legion had been stationed there since 117/118. It is unclear whether Marcus made Carnuntum his base of operations in 170; it was in 171, and would be his headquarters at various points until 179. If it was Marcus' base in 170, then the Roman defeat at Carnuntum was even more disastrous than any source admits; it also makes Marcus' quick recovery all the more remarkable. The loss at Carnuntum was Rome's greatest defeat in more than a century (Elliott 2020: 108). Birley posits (1987: 163) that it may have been Claudius Fronto, commanding multiple provinces in Dacia, who was successful and that it was Marcus' campaign that proved disastrous for the Romans. Claudius Fronto was dead before the year was out, however, so he may have met with disaster while on campaign, as his epitaph tells us: 'after several successful battles against Germans and Iazyges, he fell, fighting for the state to the last' (*CIL* 6.41142).

The creation of the new Italian and Alpine command did not stop the invaders either, although we do not hear of the fate of Antistius Adventus or any successor. Other possibilities for Marcus' headquarters exist, however; according to van Ackeren (2012: 224) it could have been at Sirmium (modern-day Sremska Mitrovica, Serbia) on the Save (or Sava) River, or even Singidunum (modern-day Belgrade, Serbia). This was some 500km away from Carnuntum and if this was where Marcus based himself, it might provide us with a more comprehensible picture of the events of 170.

Currently on display at the National Museum of the Union, Alba-Iulia, Romania, this statue from Apulum (modern-day Alba-Iulia) shows Publius Helvius Pertinax in ceremonial armour of a style largely unchanged since the 5th century BC, with muscled cuirass and *pteruges*. Because Pertinax became emperor briefly in 193, a year in which there were five emperors, we know much more about his career as a commander under Marcus Aurelius than we would otherwise. Pertinax's reign lasted only 87 days and he was assassinated by the Praetorian Guard whom he had tried to reform. (Codrin.B/ Wikimedia/CC BY-SA 3.0)

Given the many delays in Marcus' actually marching to the front – he probably only left Rome in autumn – it is probable that there had been large-scale raids over the Danube in 169 and most of 170 (as suggested by Dio). Perhaps, as these raids proved successful and met with no effective response from Rome, even more tribe members joined their brethren, giving the invaders overwhelming numbers. If the Roman defeat at Carnuntum, the siege of Aquileia and the sacking of Opitergium were roughly concurrent, it would have taken Marcus, marching from Sirmium or Singidunum, some time to respond. We might surmise that these raids happened while Marcus was in Rome and that one reason for his grieving his son for only five days was the urgency for Marcus and his staff to get to the front. That he did this, and was then able to force the tribes back towards the Danube and into negotiations, seems to fit with what the sources tell us – the only question is: how long did all of this take?

The summary of Dio, which survives in the epitome made by the monk John Xiphilinus in the 11th century, inexplicably glosses over the loss at Carnuntum, the siege of Aquileia and the sacking of Opitergium, giving us no details and moving on very quickly to the subsequent successes of Marcus through his subordinates: 'Many of the [Germans], too, from across the [Danube], advanced as far as Italy and inflicted many injuries upon the Romans. They were in turn attacked by Marcus, who opposed to them his lieutenants Pompeianus and Pertinax; and Pertinax (who later became

A Dacian *sica* blade from the 1st century BC. A short sword or long dagger with a blade 30–40cm in length, this type of weapon had a long history, having been used by Thracian, Dacian and Illyrian peoples – although originally from the Halstatt Culture, and therefore the same territory as the Marcomanni and Quadi. Such weapons can be seen on reliefs of the Marcomannic Wars as well as on Trajan's Column. This example is now in the National Museum of Romanian History, Bucharest, Romania. (Dorieo/Wikimedia/CC BY-SA 4.0)

emperor) greatly distinguished himself. Among the corpses of the barbarians there were found even women's bodies in armour' (Dio, 71/72.3.2).

Xiphilinus uses the terms 'Celts' and 'Rhine' rather than 'Germans' and 'Ister'/'Danube' – the former was a common way of referring to Germanic tribes and he has simply got his river wrong; the other sources use Ister. 'Many injuries' is all the detail we get from Dio, and the focus is then on the Romans' recovery from the disaster (although Dio does not admit there was a disaster in the first place). While we do not know how much more detail was provided in Dio's original, we can note that this summary is not quite the same as the picture given in Ammianus, in which Marcus' victories were only achieved 'with difficulty' (29.6.1).

The *SHA*'s life of Pertinax provides some more detail. Publius Helvius Pertinax would rise to be emperor briefly in 193, but came from humble origins, possibly even being the son of a slave. The mention of him with Pompeianus here implies that this passage (*SHA, Pertinax* 2.1–4) relates to this period. It tells us that Pertinax served in the Parthian War and was then transferred to Britain, going on to command the German fleet. His career and string of commands look remarkably similar to those of Maximianus. Pertinax was transferred to Dacia, where 'through the machinations of certain persons he came to be distrusted by Marcus and was removed from this post' (*SHA, Pertinax* 2.4). This was probably when Calpurnius Agricola died and when, soon after, Claudius Fronto took over from Pertinax's command as well (Birley 1987: 161). We are then told that 'afterwards, however, through the influence of Claudius Pompeianus, the son-in-law of Marcus, he was detailed to the command of detachments on the plea that he would become Pompeianus' aide' (*SHA, Pertinax* 2.4). Originally from Syria and of obscure origins – his father was not a senator although he had risen to be prefect of Egypt, personally appointed by the emperor – Claudius Pompeianus had become Marcus' chief military adviser. In 167 Pompeianus was governor of Pannonia Inferior and, despite Pompeianus being about 50 years old in 170, Marcus married him to his daughter Lucilla, Verus' 19-year-old widow. Pompeianus accompanied Marcus when he left Rome for the front, late in 170, September at the earliest. We have the issue of coinage depicting the *profectio*, the emperor's official departure from Rome and others have the *adlocutio*, the emperor addressing his troops and the usual mark of the beginning of a campaign (*BMC, RE* 4.1425, 1371, 1372).

Later in 170 (very late in the campaigning season), or early in 171, would seem to be the moment when Pompeianus and Pertinax are mentioned commanding together in Dio. Pertinax's command of 'detachments' is also of interest – these would be vexillations of various units and, given the Roman manpower shortage that led to the recruitment of diverse groups, perhaps some of these newly raised troops in an ad hoc command. It is possible that Pertinax's fall from grace was in some way connected with the disaster at Carnuntum or other concurrent invasions, but this is unclear. There was disruption in Dacia at the same time, as a chieftain named Tarbus had invaded Dacia (Dio, 71/72.3.11). Elliott posits (2020: 110) that the operations undertaken by Pertinax and Pompeianus did not take place until 171, time enough for Pertinax to be brought back into favour, perhaps – and he may have continued in command until 174 (see below).

The Battle on the Ice

AD 172

BACKGROUND TO BATTLE

After the Roman defeat at Carnuntum and the other setbacks of 170, the summary of Cassius Dio states that 'a mighty struggle had taken place and a brilliant victory had been won' (71/72.3.3–4). Presumably, this 'victory' relates to the recovery of the Roman territory lost during the previous year. The soldiers requested a donative, but it was refused; there was still work to do (and funds were short). We know that Salona, the chief city of Dalmatia, was provided with fortifications in 170 (*ILS* 2287; *CIL* 3.1979), undertaken by the men of the new legions, *II* and *III Italica*, as well as four new Dalmatian cohorts (van Ackeren 2012: 225).

Dio continues (71/72.3.11–12) that the emperor remained in Pannonia and there gave audience to the barbarians. Several offered to become Roman allies and provide troops for the impending expedition across the Danube. The Quadi asked for peace and this was granted; in return, the Quadi provided 'many horses and cattle and promised to surrender all the deserters and the captives' (Dio, 71/72.3.11). Another indication of the seriousness of the Roman losses of 170 is the claim that the Quadi initially handed over 13,000 captives and deserters 'and later all the others as well' (Dio, 71.72.3.11). Many of these soldiers – those who were fit for service – were returned to duty.

Other tribes and nations also offered surrender or alliance. These included: the Astingi (or Hasdingi), a Vandal people under their chieftains Raüs and Raptus; the Lacringi; and a confederation led by Battarius, a 12-year-old boy-king. We are told, somewhat vaguely, that 'some of them were sent on campaign elsewhere' (Dio, 71/72.3.11). The tribes offering such service usually demanded money and land to settle. We are told that the various new allies of Rome received land in Dacia, Pannonia, Moesia, the provinces

The Column of Marcus Aurelius, still *in situ*, dominates the Piazza Colonna in Rome. Although some of the scenes have been damaged, there is still an immense amount of detail to be gleaned from many of them, even though we have no closely corresponding historical or literary sources. There may be enough, however – such as in the Miracle of the Rain – to show that they did fit an actual narrative of the campaigns. (Matthias Kabel/Wikimedia/ CC BY-SA 3.0)

of Germania and even in Italy, settled near Ravenna. In many cases, these offers of alliance to the Romans were made in order to settle old scores with neighbouring peoples or traditional enemies. Even the Lacringi turned on and defeated the Astingi within Roman territory (Dio, 71/72.3.12). In some cases, these tribes would prove fruitful and useful Roman allies, but we are also told of other promises that were not fulfilled, such as that made by the Cotini, who promised to join a campaign against the Marcomanni but failed to do so and treated the Roman representative, Publius Tarrutenius Paternus, shamefully (Dio, 71/72.3.12).

As already mentioned, the *SHA* tells us that the Romans 'overwhelmed the Marcomanni while they were crossing the Danube' (*Marcus* 21.10). This statement was probably intended to relate to the events of late 171 or early 172; the latter was the year that Marcus took the title *Germanicus* (*CIL* 3.1450). In 171 he was acclaimed *imperator* ('victorious commander') for the sixth time. Coins of that year show Marcus and his soldiers crossing a river with the inscription *virtus Aug*[*usti*] ('virtue of the Augustus'). This probably marked the beginning of a new campaign (van Ackeren 2012: 226). Other coins have the legend *Germania Subacta* ('Germania Subdued' – although *subacta* means 'cultivated', so the meaning is more civilizing) or *Vic*[*toria*] *Ger*[*mania*] ('Victory over Germania') (*BMC RE* 4.563, 1453–57). The *SHA* relates that Marcus restored the plunder that had been taken to its rightful owners; if this detail relates to the sack of Opitergium and the pursuit of the Marcomanni laden down with plunder from that city, it does imply a rapid response from Marcus. The *SHA* then gives us a useful summary: 'Then, from the borders of Illyricum even into Gaul, all the nations banded together against us – the Marcomanni, Varistae, Hermunduri and Quadi, the Suebians, Sarmatians, Lacringes and Buri, these and certain others together with the Victuali, namely, Osi, Bessi, Cobotes, Roxolani, Bastarnae, Alani, Peucini, and finally, the Costoboci. Furthermore, war threatened in Parthia and Britain' (*Marcus* 22.1). Having given us this, the *SHA* then reverts to its usual much less useful material: 'Thereupon, by immense labour on his own part, while his soldiers reflected his energy, and both legates and prefects of the guard led the host, he conquered these exceedingly fierce peoples, accepted the surrender of the Marcomanni, and brought a great number of them to Italy' (*Marcus* 22.2).

We must, again, turn to our other sources for more detail. The Costoboci, usually resident north of Dacia, ravaged the Balkans – they reached Athens, but did not take it. These incursions may have occurred in 170 – and been the cause of Claudius Fronto's death – or in 171. Like Pompeianus and Pertinax in Italy and Pannonia, a procurator, Vehilius Gratus Julianus, was sent to deal with the situation in Macedonia and Achaea; Valerius Maximianus used his detachments of marines with cavalry there too. There were rebellions in Egypt (Dio, 71/72.4.1–2) and Baetica in Spain; all were dealt with by trusted subordinates – Aufidius Victorinus in Spain and Avidius Cassius in Egypt (although the latter would usurp the throne).

In 172, the Roman offensive into the land of the Marcomanni was finally launched. One of the rare surviving fragments of Dio's account (as opposed to a summary) tells us just how the Romans bridged rivers. This passage is particularly useful because it corresponds to Scene 3 on the Column of Marcus Aurelius:

The ships by means of which the river is to be bridged are flat-bottomed, and these are anchored a little way up-stream from the spot where the bridge is to be constructed. Then, when the signal is given, they first let one ship drift down-stream close to the bank that they are holding; and when it has come opposite to the spot that is to be bridged, they throw into the stream a wicker-basket filled with stones and fastened by a cable, which serves as an anchor. Made fast in this way, the ship remains in position near the bank, and by means of planks and bridge-work, which the vessel carries in large quantity, a floor is at once laid to the landing-place. Then they send down another ship at a little distance from the first, and another one beyond that, until they have extended the bridge to the opposite bank. The ship that is nearest the enemy's bank carries towers upon it and a gate and archers and catapults. (Dio, 71.3)

Other passages in Dio's summary are less useful and difficult to place chronologically, one telling us: 'When the Marcomanni were successful in a certain battle and slew Marcus Vindex, the prefect, the emperor erected three statues in his honour; and after conquering the foe he himself received the title of Germanicus' (71/72.3.5). These events probably date to late 171 or 172, as that was when the title was mentioned on coins. This anecdote also shows that, even on the offensive, the Romans did not have it all their own way. We then get a rather disjointed comment in Dio that: 'it was during Marcus' war against the Germans that the following incidents occurred (I hope these anecdotes may be thought worthy of record)' (71/72.5.1). This collection of anecdotes (as summarized) includes both the Battle on the Ice and the Miracle of the Rain, although there is very little context given in the text itself and varying chronological reconstructions of the campaigns have been advocated at various points in time.

Scene 3 of the Column of Marcus Aurelius shows the crossing of the Danube on a river of boats, as described by Dio and shown on coins. This would seem to date the beginning of the column's narrative to 172, when the crossing was first made, although it may date from later in the campaign instead. Various types of armour can be seen and Marcus himself, depicted on foot and slightly larger than the men around him, leads the men across. Marcus is shown on the column 62 separate times. (INTERFOTO/Alamy Stock Photo)

MAP KEY

1 Crossing the frozen Danube in search of plunder, the lazyges and their Quadi allies have looted the local area and returned towards their territory near its border with the lands of the Quadi, in the vicinity of Aquincum. Hoping to lure the Roman garrison into pursuing them and becoming encircled and trapped on the frozen river, the lazyges and Quadi intend to defeat the emperor's soldiers with a force of mixed cavalry and infantry (**A**) with experience of moving on the ice.

2 The Roman garrison from Aquincum responds as expected, pursuing the lazyges and Quadi on to the frozen river. The Roman force, some 20,000 men, is made up of both legions (**B**) and auxiliary units consisting of *cohortes peditatae* (**C**), *cohortes equitatae* (**D**) and cavalry *alae* (**E**). The two legions deploy in two lines with the first cohort on the right in each (**F**). To their left are the second cohort (**G**), then the third (**H**), then the fourth (**I**), and the fifth makes up the left (**J**). The second Roman line consists of the sixth cohort on the right

(**K**), then the seventh (**L**), eighth (**M**) and ninth (**N**), with the tenth (**O**) on the left of the second line. Behind the legions and on the flanks are the auxiliary infantry and, behind them, the cavalry *alae*.

3 Once the Roman force is fully committed and is completely on the ice, the lazyges turn-about and charge the Roman forces, while some of the tribesmen seek to encircle the Romans. The Roman commander orders that his legions form a compact body, with some of the men in the front rank standing on their shields. By doing this, the Romans are able to withstand the initial charge of the lazyges and Quadi.

4 With their initial charge spent, and with missiles from the Roman auxiliaries peppering them, the lazyges and Quadi break and flee for the northern bank of the Danube. The Roman auxiliary cavalry are unleashed to chase down the defeated foe.

Battlefield environment

Given that the battlefield was the frozen Danube, we might expect that some lucky archaeological find on the riverbed has been uncovered or dredged up to reveal artefacts suggesting the battle site. Alas, none has. What is more, the account of the battle places emphasis upon what happened and how unusual it was, but does not make it clear where it occurred.

There are some clues, however. We know the warriors facing the Romans were predominantly tribesmen of the lazyges (although some accounts tell of allies) and the Quadi could have invited them to attack the Romans. This might suggest a location on the Danube close to the boundary of the lands of the Quadi and their neighbours, the lazyges, although

their territory ran along the entire eastern boundary of Pannonia Inferior. Such a location might be close to Aquincum.

The frozen state of the river suggests that the battle should be placed early in the year, when the Danube was still frozen solid. Marcus' taking the title of *Germanicus* later in the year also implies that the battle took place early that year. What information we have on the climate conditions suggests that the Danube froze in January and February, sometimes for a month, sometimes two. The ice could be more than 2m thick (accounts say it froze to the bottom) and the temperature could plunge below -20°C, sometimes almost to -40°C.

A view of the ruins of Aquincum (in modern-day Budapest, Hungary), where Marcus probably wrote book 1 or 2 of his *Meditations*. Along with Sirmium, Aquincum was the capital of Pannonia Inferior and also the staging post for campaigns against the lazyges, who occupied the opposite bank of the Danube. Of the various options available to the Romans, Aquincum was closest to lazyges territory, which itself bordered on that of the Quadi. (iStock/Getty Images Plus)

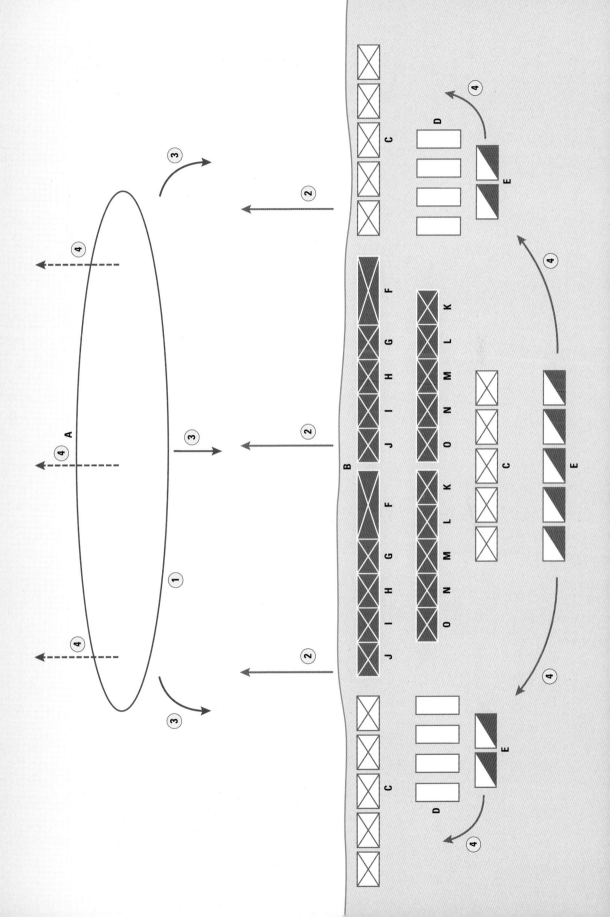

INTO COMBAT

The summary of Cassius Dio occurs in two passages (71/72.7 and 71/72.13–14). Although this is all we have to go on and any reconstruction of the campaign is speculative, much can be inferred from Dio's anecdotal account. He tells us: 'The Iazyges were conquered by the Romans on land at this time and later on the river. By this I do not mean that any naval battle took place, but that the Romans pursued them as they fled over the frozen Ister and fought there as on dry land' (71/72.7). The question is, was this part of an expedition into Iazyges territory, suggested by 'conquered by the Romans on land', or was it a raid by the Iazyges over the frozen Danube, suggesting it was either very late in the campaigning season or early the following year?

The latter scenario seems more likely. In which case, the Iazyges raid was defeated on land on the Roman side of the Danube and, as the Iazyges and their allies retreated, they were pursued onto the frozen river. What is more, Dio tells us (71/72.13) that the Iazyges had the Quadi as their allies at this time, so this was a concerted raid. This point also would seem to place the punishment of the Quadi after the Battle on the Ice. Marcus' *Meditations* may offer some help too. At the end of Book 2, we find a statement of where it was written. This possibly should be attached to the following book, however. Book 1 was written 'among the Quadi on the Granua' (1.17.8) and Book 2 at Carnuntum (2.17). The Granua River (the modern-day Hron, Slovakia) was a tributary of the Danube near the intersection of the lands of the Quadi and Sarmatians. Marcus was in Carnuntum in June 172 (*AE* 1982.778), but

Now in the Budapest History Museum, Hungary, this terracotta mould from Aquincum was used to produce tablets or medallions; it depicts the emperor Marcus Aurelius driving a chariot with Victory by his side. He drives underneath a triumphal arch proceeded by a man in armour (possibly the god Mars). The emperor strikes at a barbarian behind the chariot. Below the scene and above the arch, various types of weapon and shield are depicted. (Bjoertvedt/Wikimedia/ CC BY-SA 4.0)

A depiction of the Sarmatians as heavily armoured cavalry (*cataphractarii*) on Trajan's Column; this illustration is taken from Plate XXVIII in Conrad Cichorius's book *Die Reliefs der Traianssäule*, published by Verlag von Georg Reimer, Berlin, in 1896. Nothing in the surviving descriptions – or on the Column of Marcus Aurelius – shows them as such. Indeed, on the frozen Danube, such heavy troops would have been a liability. (Gun Powder Ma/ Wikimedia/Public Domain)

his base for campaigns on the Granua may have been Aquincum. Given the frozen state of the river, and the title of *Germanicus* taken by Marcus later in the year, we should place the Battle on the Ice in early 172 rather than late.

The will to fight had not completely gone from the Iazyges, however, and theirs was not a headlong flight. The summary of Dio continues: 'The Iazyges, perceiving that they were being pursued, awaited their opponents' onset, expecting to overcome them easily, as the others were not accustomed to the ice' (71/72.7). This might also suggest a feigned retreat by the Iazyges, luring their Roman pursuers onto the ice. What happened next certainly suggests that this was part of the Iazyges' plan, using superior numbers of more mobile and lighter-armed troops to surround the heavily equipped Roman infantrymen on the ice.

Next, Dio tells us that 'some of the barbarians dashed straight at them, while others rode round to attack their flanks, as their horses had been trained to run safely even over a surface of this kind' (71/72.7). The Roman force was surrounded, just as Marcus' forces probably were at Carnuntum and as they would be again before the Miracle of the Rain. In this instance, and probably due to superior Roman leadership – or at least leadership that remained calm in the face of potential calamity – 'the Romans upon observing this were not alarmed, but formed in a compact body (*sustraphentes*), facing all their foes at once, and most of them laid down their shields and rested one foot upon them, so that they might not slip so much; and thus they received the enemy's charge' (Dio, 71/72.7). The use of the term *sustraphentes*, meaning 'to gather together into one body', suggests that the Roman pursuit was in

Marcus Valerius Maximianus

The career of Marcus Valerius Maximianus is recorded in two inscriptions, one set up in Laugaricio (modern-day Trenčin, Slovakia) in 179 (*CIL* 3.13439) and another, longer inscription, set up in North Africa at Diana Veteranorum (modern-day Ain Zana, Algeria: *AE* 1956.124). He is not mentioned in any surviving literary source.

Maximianus, a wealthy equestrian from Poetovio (modern-day Ptuj, Slovenia) in Pannonia, was first made prefect of the *cohors I Thracum* and then tribune of the *cohors I Hamiorum*. He was rewarded for his service in the Parthian War and then selected for the Germanic War, with the special task of bringing supplies via the Danube to supply Pannonia Superior and Inferior. For this, he was placed in command of detachments of the fleets at Misenum, Ravenna and Britannia as well as having African and Moorish cavalry for scouting in Pannonia, perhaps to ensure that the supplies could be kept safe.

In Germania, Maximianus was then promoted prefect of the *ala I Hispanorum Aravacorum*, an auxiliary cavalry unit from Spain. While in command of the Aravacans, he was praised by the emperor because he personally defeated 'Valao, chief of the Naristi'. As a reward, he was given the chief's horse decorations and weapons. He was promoted to prefect of the *ala I Ulpia Contariorum*, one of the first Roman units to be armed with the *contus* (lance). Maximianus was then put in command of the cavalry of the Marcomanni, Naristi and Quadi enrolled into the Roman Army and was sent with them to Syria to put down the usurper Avidius Cassius in 175. This was the fate of some of the former belligerents who served as Roman auxiliaries.

Maximianus was then made procurator of Moesia Inferior and given the command of vexillations to defeat brigands operating on the borders of Macedonia and Thrace. He subsequently became procurator of Moesia Superior and Dacia Porolissensis, and was then adlected to the senate. Soon after that he was made *legatus* of the *legio I Adiutrix*, then *legio II Adiutrix* at its winter quarters at Laugaricio. This can be dated to 179, based on the second inscription, which suggests a rapid number of commands and promotions during (and before) 175–79. He was exactly the kind of leader Rome needed during this dangerous period for the empire.

---

relatively open order but, when the enemy turned and charged, the Romans formed into a single compact unit. This was probably a predetermined plan and something the Roman infantry needed to do to avoid annihilation at the hands of a faster enemy that included cavalry. We are not told that this was a *testudo* formation; Dio describes that formation earlier elsewhere (49.29.2–31.1), using the term *chelone*, Greek for 'tortoise', so would have presumably used the same description again. Such a formation can be seen on the Column of Marcus Aurelius (Scene 54), but in the context of storming an enemy fortification and not in open battle. In their compact formation, some Romans

> seized the bridles, others the shields and spearshafts of their assailants, and drew the men toward them; and thus, becoming involved in close conflict, they knocked down both men and horses, since the barbarians by reason of their momentum could no longer keep from slipping. The Romans, to be sure, also slipped; but in case one of them fell on his back, he would drag his adversary down on top of him and then with his feet would hurl him backwards, as in a wrestling match, and so would get on top of him; and if one fell on his face, he would actually seize with his teeth his antagonist, who had fallen first. For the barbarians, being unused to a contest of this sort, and having lighter equipment, were unable to resist, so that but few escaped out of a large force. (Dio, 71/72.7)

After their defeat, Dio tells us (71/72.13) that envoys from the Iazyges were sent to Marcus to request peace, but that this was refused – in part because Marcus knew they were untrustworthy and secondly because the Quadi had

There is not enough detail in the sources to reconstruct the biography of a single Germanic commander or warrior. There are, however, enough details across our sources to give us some clues. Named individuals are rare; across the entire Marcomannic Wars we are given the names of only a few leaders of the various tribes.

Ballomar is mentioned in the actions prior to 170, but his name soon disappears. We presume, in the absence of another named ruler for the Marcomanni, that he continued in that role and that the determination to punish and subdue them was due to his leadership and the acts and betrayal of his word he had perpetrated as leader.

Using what we know of Germanic tribes (partly from Tacitus), we are given some other leadership models for various tribes, such as the 12-year-old Battarius. He led the Lacringi and a confederation of tribes, although we are not told which, or how many; they promised to be allies of the Romans, no doubt promising to serve as auxiliaries in which capacity they were able to restrain a certain chieftain Tarbus who had invaded Dacia. Elsewhere we are told of Valerius Maximianus defeating Valao, chief of the Naristi who then provided 3,000

auxiliaries (perhaps six cohorts). Another inscription names Peiporus, king of the Costoboci, but it is unclear if he is associated with the activities of the Costoboci during Marcus' wars.

We have the detail of the Astingi tribe, led by the brothers Raüs and Raptus, who also entered Dacia, looking to secure both money and land in return for their alliance: that is, providing auxiliaries. This brother co-chieftainship reminds us of the later tradition we find with the leadership of the Huns before Attila. We also know of the Quadi expelling their king, Furtius, perhaps to placate the Romans and then installing an alternative, Ariogaesus, who was not accepted by Marcus.

All of these types of leadership imply that Tacitus' simplistic idea that rule of the Germanic tribes was achieved by strength does not reflect the complex systems by which men (and boys) came to be recognized as rulers, maintained their rule or were replaced. Securing money, land and alliance (usually by providing auxiliaries) seems to have been a relatively consistent element of these rulers' relationships with Rome no matter who was in command.

deceived him and he now wished to destroy them utterly. (This statement looks ahead to the expedition to punish the Quadi, which would come in 174.) The Quadi had received a separate peace in 171, but had apparently taken in Marcomanni fugitives. We are also told that the Quadi had not handed over all their Roman captives (from the battle of Carnuntum) as they had promised to do. The only prisoners they did hand over were those they could not sell as slaves or force to do labour. Those in good physical condition who were released found their relatives were kept prisoner as a guarantee that they would desert the Roman cause and rejoin the Quadi. This would seem to refer to Germanic tribesmen who had been employed by Rome against their fellow Germans and whose families had been taken as part of the Quadi plunder.

The Quadi, probably as an act of appeasement, expelled their king, Furtius, and 'on their own responsibility' (Dio, 71/72.13) appointed a new king, one Ariogaesus. Marcus refused to recognize this choice, thereby implying that an alternate candidate needed to be vetted by Rome in order to be acceptable to any peace process. Birley posits (1987: 177) that Furtius was a pro-Roman king, but this ignores the point that the Quadi had allied with the Iazyges. The Quadi may have been desperate, because they offered to surrender 50,000 captives (either prisoners or their own men to fight as auxiliaries) if Marcus would accept peace and Ariogaesus' kingly status. Dio goes on, however, to tell us (71/72.14) that Marcus remained bitter towards Ariogaesus and even put a price on his head, to be delivered to him alive or dead; the reward would be doubled if he was delivered alive. We are not given

The tombstone of a Praetorian guardsman, dating from the early 2nd century AD. It was found in Pozzuoli, Italy, and is now in the Pergamon Museum, Berlin, Germany. Note the thrusting spear (*hasta*) like those shown on the Column of Marcus Aurelius; the flat, oval shield; the *gladius* on the right hip and the small *balteus*. Another near-contemporary sculpture from Croy Hill in Scotland shows a legionary with a curved rectangular *scutum*. (Magnus Manske/ Wikimedia/CC BY-SA 3.0)

any further detail, but are told that when Ariogaesus was later captured alive, he was not harmed but sent to Alexandria. This was probably later, after the punitive expedition into Quadi territory, although it is possible that chapters 7 and 13 are not connected so that the attempt at peace came later (and the Miracle of the Rain is recounted in chapters 8–10, but these are usually placed after chapter 14). Confusingly, the ordering of the fragments and summaries of Dio differs in various editions.

Birley (1987: 177) dates the Battle on the Ice to a campaign in winter 173/74 or 174/75, but he reminds us that virtually nothing is known of the campaign, surmising that Dio's account is a curiosity. Dio gives us a brief summary, stating that Marcus fought 'with both the Iazyges and the Marcomanni, one after the other, using Pannonia as his base' (71/72.3), which suggests the Romans fought the Iazyges before they faced the Marcomanni in 172. Birley sums up that the Iazyges had 'obviously' attempted a surprise attack, but were repelled and retreated over the ice. It was one instance in the wars in which Roman defences held. In other cases, Roman successes came only on the offensive; the incursions over a succession of years showed the Romans' initial reaction and defences to be deficient. This situation would not improve for the empire, as the successful barbarian invasions of the next three centuries would show.

Unlike the accounts of the battle of Carnuntum, in which we are not told of enemy cavalry, here the use of Iazyges cavalry is made explicit. It is therefore pertinent to apply the *Ektaxis kat' Alanon* of Flavius Arrian. The Alans were a mainly cavalry-based army, even sometimes identified as Sarmatians (Marcian, *Periplus maris exteri* 2.39), and possibly shared their origins with the Iazyges (Campbell 2022: 14), so it may have been the Roman policy of the time to deploy armies against them in just such a way.

Arrian's fascinating work has only recently had a full-length study dedicated to it (Campbell 2022). After holding the consulship in 129, Arrian was governor of Cappadocia until 137, probably for a six-year term. The *Ektaxis kat' Alanon* describes the deployment of the garrison of Cappadocia, consisting of two legions (*legio XII Fulminata* and *legio XV Apollinaris*) and various units of auxiliaries against a foreign threat from a mounted enemy, the Alans. The text describes both a marching order (1–10) and a battle deployment (11–24). The beginning and end of the manuscript are lost, but the work is immensely useful for a battle order against a similar enemy only a few years before Marcus' wars. Assuming that the treatise reflects marching

The sense of scale of the span of the Danube is shown here. With the river frozen and the Sarmatians and their allies apparently fleeing, the Romans pursued them on to the ice. This may well have been part of the raiders' plan since the Romans would not usually take advantage of the frozen river but wait to build a bridge of their own. (Pavel Gospodinov/Getty Images)

and deployment doctrine of some kind, rather than being a record of a unique formation, it is highly unlikely that the doctrine Arrian reveals had changed in the meantime.

What exact purpose the text had has been a matter of debate; it could be a description, a handbook or a history. It seems to have been a set of instructions, but written by Arrian and addressed to himself (he refers to himself as 'Xenophon'). It may be a literary exercise, modelled on Xenophon's philosophical treatise of the 4th century BC, the *Cyropaedia*; Arrian refers to hoplites and phalanxes despite describing Roman formations. Nevertheless, for all its archaizing and literary affectations – Arrian lived in the middle of the Second Sophistic, when couching almost anything in terms of Greek culture was at its height (Campbell 2022: 11) – the text describes the deployment of a Roman army in the mid-2nd century AD.

The *Ektaxis kat' Alanon* gives us what histories often do not: the combination of legions and auxiliary units deployed in concert. Using this, we can extrapolate that the units in Marcus' armies (and many other imperial armies) used both legions and auxiliary units. The latter are seldom mentioned in histories, but are abundantly referenced in inscriptions of individual soldiers' careers. We do not get the intricate detail of Arrian's list for any armies in other campaigns, but he lists the troops of four cavalry wings, an infantry cohort, four part-mounted cohorts (*equitatae*), and the cavalry from four others (see Campbell 2022: 59 for details of precisely which units). These were all part of the garrison of Cappadocia, so an army on campaign could have had more, and an even greater array of units deployed. Josephus (*Jewish War* 3.115–26, 5.47–49) is the only other author to give us this much detail of the marching order of an imperial Roman army, and those from the years AD 67 and 70 respectively. Arrian has an unusual number of cavalry, although the number of cavalry units attested in the inscriptions for Marcus Aurelius' wars suggests he too had many cavalry, perhaps to chase the Germanic raiders, although the core force was still heavy infantry. Arrian lists many archer units too, which are not in evidence for Marcus' wars.

The Battle on the Ice, AD 172

Although details of the expedition against the Iazyges are slight, in early 172, while the Danube was still frozen, the Iazyges launched an invasion into Roman territory, probably at the invitation of their neighbours and allies, the Quadi – here we have depicted Quadi allies fighting by the Iazyges' side. They were pursued by Roman forces, but the lightly armed Iazyges and Quadi have crossed back onto the frozen river, luring the heavily equipped and slower Roman forces on to the ice in pursuit. When the Romans have come far enough on to the ice, the Iazyges and Quadi have turned and engaged them, hoping to break up their formation in a determined charge. Led decisively, the Romans have quickly formed into a compact body, some placing their shields on the ice to stand upon. They prepare to receive the enemy charge, knowing that in hand-to-hand fighting they have the advantage. In addition, auxiliary missile troops prepare to shoot over the compact legions protecting their front. The Iazyges and Quadi charge will waste its momentum, and they will be defeated in a slippery wrestling match on the frozen Danube.

This sarcophagus, currently in the Museo Pio-Clementino, Vatican Museums, Vatican City, Italy, shows the submission of Germanic prisoners. They are usually identified as Sarmatians, although what distinguishes them from other Germans is difficult to pinpoint; the man bowing to the seated bearded figure seems to wear a Sarmatian cap. Similar caps can be seen in the upper scenes of the Column of Marcus Aurelius. The sources relate that Romans could not necessarily tell different Germanic and Sarmatian tribes apart. (Jean-Pol GRANDMONT/Wikimedia/ CC BY 3.0)

Arrian deploys his force for battle in the following manner. His two legions are deployed eight ranks deep on the level ground, providing a frontage of approximately 1,300 men. Earlier under the Principate, legions would normally deploy in either three or six ranks (Macdowall 2013: 13). Behind these Arrian places infantry and archers from his auxiliary units. This is unusual as such missile troops are usually considered to have been deployed in front of legionary troops. Other units of auxiliary infantry and missile troops are deployed on the flanks. The cavalry forces – four complete wings and eight contingents of cavalry from eight auxiliary cohorts – are kept in reserve. These cavalry are in two groups, one on each flank behind the infantry there. Catapults are also deployed, behind the legions and on the flanks.

This is the most detailed description of any Roman imperial army deployed for battle. We do not know whether Roman armies were normally deployed in a similar manner, although given the variety of enemies faced, terrain and other factors, it is unlikely. If this was a deployment specifically for use against cavalry foes, we might take it in combination with Vegetius'

two-line deployment in other contexts seen above. Other descriptions of deployments – such as at the battle of Mons Graupius in AD 83 (Tacitus, *Agricola* 35.2) or the battle of Cremona in AD 69 (Tacitus, *Histories* 3.21) – lack the detail we have here. What is more, those Roman armies were attacking formations. Arrian's deployment was defensive and intended to stand fast against a predominantly mounted foe such as the Alans. This may, therefore, have been similar to the deployment used by Marcus' commanders against the Sarmatians although, there, the transition from pursuit to defence was necessarily rapid.

Arrian's deployment was intended to defeat a charging mass of enemy cavalry; the legions would provide an immovable bloc of infantry over whom, and from the flanks of which, auxiliary archers would fire an inordinate number of missiles (*Ektaxis kat' Alanon* 26) to defeat the enemy. The cavalry could then launch themselves from the safety of the immobile legions. This was not a normal use of the legions, which were usually used as an attacking force. One of the strengths of the legions, however, was their flexibility, and the legionaries' armour and shields surely could, if required, provide just such a defensive bloc. One modern historian suggests (MacDowall 2013: 15-16) that the defensive nature of Arrian's deployment would have suited oval shields since, even when overlapped, this would leave a small gap for swords, *pila* or *hastae* to be thrust through. Unfortunately, Arrian does not specify what kinds of *scuta* his men had – for many Romans a shield was a shield.

Although we are not given precise details in the summary of Dio about units of Roman infantry, or auxiliary cavalry or archers, the description of the legions' behaviour on the ice seems to be similar: they met the enemy charge, but they did not advance to meet it. The detail of legionaries standing on their shields to be more secure seems to be the reason the anecdote has been preserved, but it too reveals the legions' flexibility and the use of expedient measures to meet any threat. The legions fighting in 172 may therefore have operated in a very similar way to that described by Arrian only 35 years earlier.

For the purposes of illustrating the Roman battle array, I have chosen to depict the force on the ice as similar to the army described by Arrian: two legions supported by an equal number of auxiliary forces, some 20,000 men. The only change is that the troops on the wings are drawn back slightly to prevent encirclement; whereas Arrian's array filled the valley floor, the flanks of the Romans deployed on the ice were open. The Sarmatians too may have intentionally lured the Romans on to the ice in order to disrupt their formation and, perhaps, surround them. Auxiliary units, which Marcus undoubtedly had with the army – just as he would have had artillery; each legion seems to have had a number of catapults and ballistae assigned to them – could have used the stolid, immoveable legions as a shield, just as Arrian's did, and fire a large number of missiles into the Sarmatian and Quadi ranks. We do get a description of just such a battle in AD 194 in Dio (75.7.2–4), in which the legions were positioned in front with the lightly armed auxiliaries stationed behind them and shooting over the legions. It is entirely possible that this was the formation intended in 172, especially if the Sarmatians fought as the Alans did – which seems highly likely.

This bronze *sestertius* of Marcus Aurelius, minted in Rome in 172/73 to celebrate the Roman victory in the North (*BMC RE* 4.1455), bears the legend 'M ANTONINVS AVG PR P XXVII' and, on the reverse within a laurel wreath, 'VICT/GERMA/ IMP.VI/COS III/S C'. (CNG/ Wikimedia/CC BY-SA 2.5)

The Miracle of the Rain

AD 174

BACKGROUND TO BATTLE

As has become evident, the chronology for the Marcomannic Wars is somewhat confused and open to interpretation. The reconstruction I have followed places the Miracle of the Rain after the Battle on the Ice, although the opposite reconstruction is possible and has been made (Birley 1987: 171–77). Some place both the Battle on the Ice and the Miracle of the Rain in 172, whereas Birley reverses them from the order I have postulated, placing the Miracle of the Rain in 172 and the Battle on the Ice in 174. The limitations of the sources allow any of these reconstructions.

Once more, the brief summary in the *SHA Marcus* may be useful. The author writes (*Marcus* 22.5) of the harsh military discipline Marcus oversaw, as a result of his philosophical beliefs and lifestyle for which he was criticized. He was also encouraged to abandon the Marcomannic Wars when the fighting resulted in the loss of so many lives:

> And because in this German, or Marcomannic, war, or rather I should say in this 'War of Many Nations' [*bello immo plurimarum gentium*], many nobles perished, for all of whom he erected statues in the Forum of Trajan, his friends often urged him to abandon the war and return to Rome. He, however, disregarded this advice and stood his ground, nor did he withdraw before he had brought all the wars to a conclusion. (*SHA, Marcus* 22.7–8)

As we have seen, the summary of Cassius Dio includes both the Battle on the Ice and the Miracle of the Rain in the same collection of notable anecdotes. Reconstructing the campaigns around them is somewhat challenging. One tool for doing so is the Column of Marcus Aurelius, also known as the

Aurelian Column. The column is 29.6m tall, sits on a 10.1m base and depicts the wars in a continuous spiralling narrative relief in 20 bands, the relief being divided into 116 scenes: more than 200m of frieze. Each of the column's 27 blocks weighs 40 tons and was hollowed out at the quarry to house a 200-step internal spiral staircase before being brought to Rome. Clearly modelled on Trajan's Colum in the Roman Forum, it is unclear when construction of the column was begun, although it was completed by 193. An inscription from that year (*CIL* 6.1585a) mentions Adrastus, the caretaker of the column. It is, however, first mentioned in a literary source only in the late 3rd century AD.

One school of thought suggests that the column was begun in 176 and relates the story of the Marcomannic Wars during the period 172–75. Another theory postulates that work commenced on the column in 180; it was intended as an honorary column to Marcus by his son Commodus and tells of the wars during 174–80. There are issues here, however. Commodus himself does not appear on the column, but he should feature if it tells the story of the wars from 178 onwards. There is no evidence that Commodus' image has been expunged as it was from the panels on the Arch of Constantine. Arguments that he is depicted in two scenes on the column (the pedestal and Scene 49) are tenuous at best (Beckmann 2011: 29–31). The best explanation seems to be that the column was begun in 176 and depicts events of the first part of the wars only, during 172–75, when Marcus was in sole command (see Beckmann 2011: 22).

In many ways the Column of Marcus Aurelius is the poor cousin to its model, the much more famous Trajan's Column, although its relationship to the latter is more complex than we might expect. What is more, there are several caveats that must be applied to using as evidence a monumental

The Roman Army on the march near the bottom of the Column of Marcus Aurelius (scenes 3 and 4). There is plenty of detail here in terms of armour and trumpets (*cornicines*), as well as the animal skins of the eagle-bearers (*aquiliferi*). There appears to be intricate detail of *lorica segmentata* as well as *squamata* and *hamata* armours. At the same time, however, some of the helmet details do not match archaeological finds; all the men carry spears, rather than javelins (*pila*); and every soldier has a curved, oval shield. These are intricately detailed. None of the men carries a marching pack (*sarcina*) of any kind, although their kit was probably transported on wagons and carts, which are depicted. (Barosaurus Lentus/Wikimedia/CC BY 3.0)

sculptural relief intended as propaganda, at least in part. Some have despaired of using it as evidence at all (Campbell 2022: vii), while others, notably Birley (1987: 178), contend that the column serves as a good commentary on the Marcomannic Wars. Others, such as Ferris (2009), Beckmann (2011) and Kovács (2009), have been able to discern and extrapolate complex and informative theses based on the column and its reliefs. The column was directly contemporary with the Marcomannic Wars and several historians and archaeologists have attempted to reconstruct the history of the campaigns from its scenes, with varying success. It can, however, be immensely useful and – used judiciously – is highly informative.

Scene 1 shows the Danube being bridged. This might suggest the start of the wars in 166, although no bridging seems to have occurred until 171/72; fighting prior to that date was characterized by the Roman Army's efforts to resist incursions into imperial provinces. Strikingly, Lucius Verus is not depicted, which suggests that work on the reliefs only began after his death. As already noted, Commodus is absent in the later scenes, which suggests that the coverage stops in 175, before Commodus' arrival at the front. This also suggests that its design was complete before Marcus' death and that Commodus, as emperor (r. 177–82), did not alter it to include himself.

There are problems with this interpretation, however. The Miracle of the Rain of 174 occurs early (scene 16), so to have reached that event with 100 scenes left to depict would suggest that the relief shows the rest of the war into 179. At scene 55 – more or less the halfway point – there seems to be a natural break, with the goddess Victoria flanked on either side by a trophy. It has been argued (Wolff 1990 and 1994) that the first half of the column shows the campaigns of 174–75 and the second half those of 178–79 (see van Ackeren 2012: 226–28).

There may be more complex factors at play here, however. The Miracle of the Rain was certainly one of the main incidents of the Marcomannic Wars and the scene showing it is clearly visible from the ground. This was probably a deliberate design choice and it may therefore be that the column does not offer a chronological narrative of events during the conflict, but rather a potted, non-chronological narrative of disconnected incidents arranged to have the greatest impact on the viewer. The incidents chosen may have been real ones – although any literary parallel for many of them has not survived – but these are not necessarily presented in a strict chronological order. What is more, there are clear parallels with Trajan's Column, which may have more to do with artistic parallels than with chronology

Dedicated by C[aius] Comat[ius] Flavinus, a soldier of the *legio XIIII Gemina Martia Victrix*, at Carnuntum *c.*213, this altar shows that the legion was not destroyed as Lucian's account might suggest. The return of prisoners mentioned in the sources might also indicate that things soon returned to some kind of normality and that the *legio XIIII* continued to serve during the remainder of the campaigns – it is also mentioned in the letter regarding the Miracle of the Rain. (Jona Lendering/CC0 1.0 Universal)

(Beckmann 2011: 28). The first scene of Trajan's Column also shows the Roman Army crossing the Danube via a boat bridge. The Column of Marcus Aurelius parallels that, as does the positioning of the Victoria scene (scene 55) and even the *testudo* scene on both columns (scene 54, notably with curved rectangular *scuta*; 70/71 on Trajan's Column). Other scenes are remarkably close: the barbarian hostage scenes (scene 25; 40 on Trajan's Column) and the *adlocutio* scenes (scene 4; 9 on Trajan's Column).

There are other historical events shown. The lightning strike on the enemy siege engine (*SHA, Marcus* 24.4) is shown in scenes 10 and 11. Scene 43, showing a Roman cavalryman chasing down an unbearded German youth, is also clearly related to a specific incident, as is the decapitation of prisoners (scenes 70–72). There might be evidence in the surviving literary sources that the decapitation of prisoners has not been emphasized, but this practice was included on the column, a decision in which Marcus surely had some say – if it was begun in 176. Scene 43 has been linked to Maximianus' killing of Valao in single combat, but surely the chief would have been depicted with a beard, otherwise there was no credit in Maximianus killing a boy. Perhaps it relates somehow to the boy-king Battarius. We see Marcus shielded from enemy slingers across the river (scene 10) and, in the only battle in which he personally appears on the column (scene 27), he is accompanied by cavalry, either the *custodes* or the *equites singulares Augustii*.

Although the Column of Marcus Aurelius does not offer a linear narrative and there are several moments of artistic licence that do not reflect the reality of Roman equipment or practice, there are, nevertheless, useful clues on the column and it does tell us something of the Marcomannic Wars – not least how Marcus himself (perhaps) wanted them to be seen.

Scene 27 of the Column of Marcus Aurelius shows Roman and Germanic tribesmen engaged in combat involving both cavalry and infantry. The limited sources imply the fighting of such actions where cavalry and infantry mixed and fought together. Again, there is attention to detail and helpful insights into shields, equipment and various armours. (Barosaurus Lentus/ Wikimedia/CC BY 3.0)

1 The Roman force, consisting of five full legions plus vexillations and auxiliaries, has been surrounded by a much larger force of the Quadi, cutting them off from drinking water with the intention of exhausting them by thirst. The legions include *I Adiutrix* (**A**), *X Gemina* (**B**), *XII Fulminata* (**C**), *XIII Gemina* (**D**), *XIIII Gemina Martia Victrix* (**E**) and vexillations of *VI Ferrata* (**F**). The Roman troops are deployed in a rough square, the auxiliary troops (**G**) inside the square.

2 The Quadi (**H**) surround the Romans on all sides, the larger force's entire strength brought to bear in multiple tribal sub-units that outnumber the Romans.

3 As the Quadi are about to close in for the final attack on the weakening Romans, a raincloud bursts over the Roman forces, giving them succour. As they slake their thirst, they fight the Quadi with renewed strength and vigour. Accompanying the rain, lightning strikes the Quadi, throwing them into confusion. The Romans defeat the now disordered Quadi.

Battlefield environment

Once again, we have very little detail on where the Miracle of the Rain may have occurred. The territory of the Quadi might imply that it was near the Granua River, where Marcus tells us he wrote Book 1 (or 2) of the *Meditations*; but it may have been further into Quadi territory. Accounts of the battle do not dwell on the location but move on to the Miracle of the Rain itself and who was responsible for it. We might look for an open area where a large Roman force could be surrounded without any source of drinking water, and one where the Quadi could deploy their overwhelming numbers in full to surround the Romans and give no hope of escape. No modern account of the Marcomannic Wars has sought to seek a site for the battle, however.

We can expect the battle to have been fought in high-summer, with the Romans exhausted by thirst. Some historians, who date the battle to 172, believe the battle to have occurred on the day on which Marcus was acclaimed *imperator* – 11 June; Birley (1987: 252) rejects this thesis. If the battle was fought at the hottest time of the year, it would have occurred in August rather than June.

The Miracle of the Rain depiction (scene 16) on the Column of Marcus Aurelius. The narrative of the rain being divinely sent was clearly disseminated early and presented on the column relief in just such a fashion. There is no thunderbolt shown here, although we can see men catching rain in their upturned shields. Interestingly, we can see a variety of armour types, with scale (*squamata*), mail (*hamata*), banded *lorica segmentata* and even some muscled cuirasses all depicted. All of the soldiers have curved oval shields, many with different blazons. The ring-helmets are peculiar; only one example exists, but has been proven to be a forgery. (Cristiano64/Wikimedia/CC BY-SA 3.0)

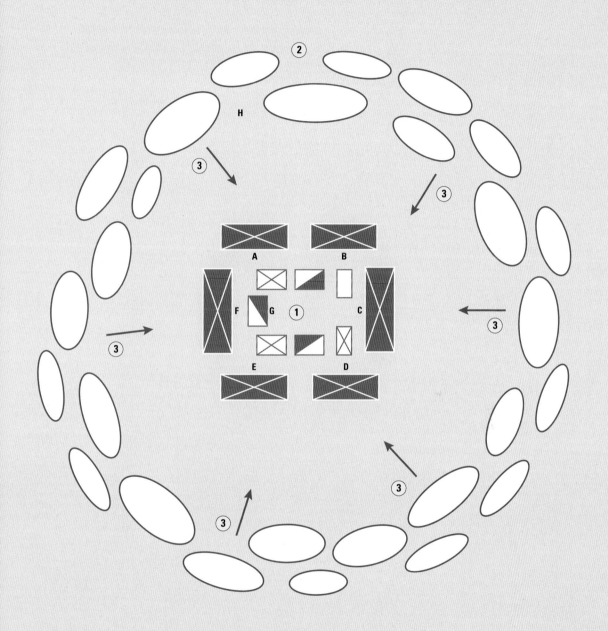

INTO COMBAT

Our main account of the battle comes in the anecdotes relating to the war summarized by John Xiphilinus (Dio, 71/72.8–10). There are, in addition, several very interesting alternative accounts that also explore the battle, although they raise more questions than they answer. According to the summary of Dio, after Marcus had subdued the Marcomanni and Iazyges 'after many hard struggles and dangers' (71/72.8), he mounted a great war against the Quadi. It was, we are told, 'his good fortune to win an unexpected victory, or rather it was vouchsafed him by Heaven. For when the Romans were in peril in the course of the battle, the divine power saved them in a most unexpected manner' (Dio, 71/72.8).

Once again, the details that follow are slight, but there are certain elements we can employ. We are told that the Quadi offered to hand over 50,000 captives to guarantee peace; this cannot have been all their manpower, however, so the idea that they had superior numbers should not surprise us.

The course of the battle can be surmised as follows. The Quadi had surrounded the Roman force on ground favourable to themselves. We are not told of the strength of the Roman force, but later accounts make it consist of a single legion (*legio XII Fulminata*). More likely it was a much larger force; Marcus seems to have been present with the army, which implies it would have consisted of many more men – and the Romans would surely have learned their lesson of having piecemeal forces surrounded and defeated as had happened throughout the course of the Marcomannic Wars. The Romans were 'fighting valiantly with their shields locked together', but the barbarians ceased fighting, 'expecting to capture them easily as the result of the heat and their thirst' (Dio, 71/72.8). The Quadi therefore posted guards around the surrounded Roman force and prevented any forays to get water. The Romans remained hemmed in, afflicted by fatigue, wounds, the heat of the sun and thirst; they could neither fight nor escape.

Suddenly, we are told, clouds gathered and 'a mighty rain, not without divine interposition, burst upon them' (Dio, 71/72.8–9). The cause of the rain preoccupied contemporary writers, but the course of the combat continued. Prior to that, however, Xiphilinus inserts himself into the summary to add material. When he returns to Dio's account of the actual combat, we read

that 'when the rain poured down, at first all turned their faces upwards and received the water in their mouths; then some held out their shields and some their helmets to catch it, and they not only took deep draughts themselves but also gave their horses to drink' (71/72.10).

Seeing this relief to their enemies, the Quadi charged them and the Romans 'drank and fought at the same time' (Dio, 71/72.10). So intent were the Romans on slaking their thirst that they should have suffered severely from the enemy's charge. At that moment, however, a violent hailstorm and 'numerous thunderbolts' fell on the ranks of the enemy (Dio, 71/72.10). The summary continues that water and fire were thus descending from the sky simultaneously. The lightning, apparently, did not touch the Romans, but only the Quadi. The Quadi fell into complete disarray, some crossing over to the seemingly safe position of the Romans. There, they were defeated utterly. The imperial victory was as total as it was unexpected. Marcus was hailed *imperator* for the seventh time and a despatch was sent to the Senate to have the honour voted upon. This may suggest a date in 174 (Beckmann 2011: 26).

This was the course of the combat, although the causes of the rain and thunder caused the most debate among our sources. Dio ascribes the rain and thunder to an Egyptian magician, Arnuphis (or Harnuphis), who was a companion of Marcus. Arnuphis invoked various deities, especially Hermes Aërios, an Egyptian god, and the Roman deity Mercury in particular to bring rain. Dio does show some scepticism by calling this 'a story to the effect', but this was insufficient for his epitomator. John Xiphilinus begins his insertion in the next sentence with the point that 'this is what Dio says about the matter, but he is apparently in error, whether intentionally or otherwise; and yet I am inclined to believe his error was chiefly intentional' (71/72.9).

John Xiphilinus goes on to point out that Dio cannot have been ignorant of the 'thundering' legion, the *legio XII Fulminata*, which, we are told, is included in the list of legions with the others (no such list was excerpted in the surviving material). The title of this legion, according to Xiphilinus, was given to it precisely because of this action. Xiphilinus also rejects the presence of Arnuphis because 'Marcus is not reported to have taken pleasure in the company of magicians or in witchcraft' (71/72.9). This seems to ignore the lengths to which Marcus had gone to previously to enlist the help of whatever religious groups he could to purify the Roman Army and allay his soldiers' fears. We saw the example of the charlatan Alexander of Abonoteichus in 170 and there is every reason to suspect that men like Arnuphis continued to accompany the Roman Army into 174, given that the plague was still rampant.

The *SHA* offers a brief and slightly different take on this battle, which may be suggestive: 'By his prayers he summoned a thunderbolt from heaven against a war-engine of the enemy, and successfully besought rain for his men when they were suffering from thirst' (*Marcus* 24.40). Birley (1987: 171–72) dates the battle to 172, arguing that a scene early on the Column of Marcus Aurelius showing Marcus carrying a thunderbolt relates to it. There is a depiction (scenes 10 and 11) of a lightning-bolt hitting a siege engine (Beckmann 2011: 133), but it is separate from the Miracle of the Rain where

Minted in 174, this coin of Marcus Aurelius depicts the emperor on horseback with his right hand outstretched. This may have been a gesture of *adlocutio*, although such scenes in sculpture and coins show the emperor on foot. He is also unarmoured. This suggests that the gesture was part of Marcus' policy – perhaps one of clemency (*clementia*), especially if the non-martial clothing was an element of it in a military context – although it is noteworthy that Marcus wears a sword on his right hip. (CNG/Wikimedia/Public Domain)

The Miracle of the Rain, AD 174

Barbarian view: Confident of victory, the overwhelming numbers of the Quadi have surrounded Marcus' men. Deprived of drinking water, the Romans have been exhausted by thirst and, although they have held out against several earlier attacks by locking their shields together, they are now at the end of their endurance. Just as the Quadi are advancing for a final assault, a raincloud has opened above the battlefield, soaking the Romans, and they drink the rainwater. Some drink from their helmets, others from their upturned shields. Some soldiers have begun to discard equipment and arms in their desperation and exhaustion. None of this deters the Quadi, who advance confidently to the attack.

Roman view: From within the ranks of the Romans of the *legio XIII Gemina*, rain beats down on the troops who welcome it to slake their thirst; they expected to die of thirst or from Quadi attacks. They are surrounded on all sides by the Quadi who close in, expecting an easy victory. Among the Romans are several candidates who would take credit for causing the rain to fall at that precise moment, in that exact spot. The Quadi advance confidently against the Romans, who are revived by the downpour. More than that, the Romans are filled with the sense that they have been saved by some kind of divine intervention and this revives their fighting spirit.

no lightning is shown. Marcus also released a series of coins in 172 showing a thunderbolt. It was, however, a relatively common motif of Roman victory and does not necessarily refer to this specific incident. The thunderbolt incident and the relief of the army by rain may, nevertheless, indicate that two separate incidents were later combined into one. It is even possible that the *SHA* reported the events depicted on the Column of Marcus Aurelius rather than independently (Beckmann 2011: 140). Marcus being the one who prayed is also pertinent to other accounts. The rain scene does show barbarian and horse casualties, but none appear to have been caused by any discernible lightning strike.

Perhaps the most remarkable aspect of the Miracle of the Rain is the responsibility claimed for the victory by Christian writers, both at the time (apparently) and subsequently. This claim was not included in Dio's original, but was added by Xiphilinus, although it had already appeared soon after the battle and even before Dio wrote his version of events; there is no reason to assume Dio had read the account in his research, however. Xiphilinus substitutes Dio's explanation for one of his own:

Now the incident I have reference to is this: Marcus had a division of soldiers (the Romans call a division a legion) from Melitene; and these people are all worshippers of Christ. Now it is stated that in this battle, when Marcus found himself at a loss what to do in the circumstances and feared for his whole army, the prefect approached him and told him that those who are called Christians can accomplish anything whatever by their prayers and that in the army there chanced to be a whole division of this sect. Marcus on hearing this appealed to them to pray to their God; and when they had prayed, their God immediately gave ear and smote the enemy with a thunderbolt and comforted the Romans with a shower of rain. Marcus was greatly astonished at this and not only honoured the Christians by an official decree but also named the legion the 'thundering' Legion. It is also reported that there is a letter of Marcus extant on the subject. But the Greeks, though they know that the division was called the 'Thundering' Legion and themselves bear witness to the fact, nevertheless make no statement whatever about the reason for its name. (Dio, 71/72.9)

Found in Somzée, Belgium, and now in the Royal Museums of Fine Arts of Belgium, Brussels (Inv. A1145), this sculpture of a Germanic head shows the Suebian knot clearly. The dating is uncertain (late 1st or 2nd century AD), but such sculptures, probably made in Italy, would have been popular during the Marcomannic Wars. On some bog bodies that may date from the period of the Marcomannic Wars, especially the Osterby Man and the Dätgen Man (named after the villages in Germany near which they were found), the hair is remarkably well preserved and was formed into a Suebian knot when the men were killed and decapitated. (Bullenwächter/Wikimedia/CC BY-SA 3.0)

It should be noted that the *legio XII* had been associated with the epithet *Fulminata* since the days of Mark Antony in the 1st century BC (*CIL* 3.7261; Parker 1958: 269), so the origin of the story as presented here is false. We do, however, apparently have a copy of the letter referred to, appended to *The First Apology of Justin Martyr* (*c*.100–*c*.168): *Marci imperatoris Epistola ad senatum, qua testatur Christianos victoriae causam fuisse* ('Letter of the emperor Marcus to the senate, in which he testifies that the Christians were the cause of the victory'). Justin was martyred in Rome, being beheaded at the behest of the urban prefect Junius Rusticus, who was only in that office during 162–68 and so is exactly contemporary to the Marcomannic Wars (although Rusticus died before the campaign of 174). There seems to be no evidence that Christians like Justin were asked to partake in the various religious attempts to purify Rome in the 160s and 170s, although it is entirely possible. The Christian religion was not unknown to the highest echelons of Roman society; even Marcus mentions the followers of Christ and shows a knowledge of their beliefs (*Meditations* 11.3). Earlier in the century, *c*.112, the governor of Bithynia, Pliny the Younger, wrote to the emperor Trajan about them too (*Letters* 10.96).

The letter preserved in Justin's writings is spurious, but was a contemporary forgery, first mentioned about 30 years later. It came to be considered factual, especially by later Christian commentators, and was the source of great debate, even though it post-dated Justin's life. It is highly unlikely that Christian soldiers were particularly numerous in the 170s, certainly not enough to contribute an entire unit; and there is no evidence of a unit from Melitene, a kingdom in Cappadocia that was annexed by Rome in AD 70 and where the *legio XII Fulminata* was stationed between that year and AD 92 (although some inscriptions do not include the epithet; sometimes they just read *Leg. XII*). Melitene was indeed an early centre of Christianity, so it is possible there were some Christian soldiers in the legion, but they certainly would not have taken credit at the time in any public way, however. The incident may have been invented subsequently, or been expanded upon, although it was circulating very soon after. The title of *Sarmaticus* by which Marcus is addressed in the letter does not seem to have been adopted until 175, so is a further proof of the letter's later invention. Tertullian (*c*.155–*c*.220), who converted to Christianity in the very late 2nd century AD, mentions the letter (*Apology* 5); that work, although impossible to date precisely, was created in the early 3rd century AD. Tertullian, speaking of emperors who did not persecute Christians, writes that when in Germany, Marcus wrote a letter stating that 'being just upon perishing with thirst, some Christian soldiers which happened to be in his troops, did by the power of prayer fetch down a prodigious shower to the relief of the whole army' (*Apology* 5).

Themistius, writing in the 4th century AD (*Oration 15* 191B-C), reported the contents of a painting showing Marcus in the front line (it is the only source to place the emperor there) with his hands raised in prayer. Themistius claims that it was Marcus who prayed – something the *SHA* also reported (*Marcus* 24.40) – and, Themistius claims, the painting showed his soldiers filling their helmets with rain.

Eusebius (*c*.260–339) also wrote of the incident in his *Ecclesiastical History* (5.5.1–6) and in his *Chronicon* (2189 = AD 173). He tells us that Pertinax was the commander of the Roman forces afflicted by thirst fighting in the land of the Quadi. A rain sent by God with lightning-bolts afflicted the Germans and Sarmatians and killed many of them (see Beckmann 2011: 138–39). Eusebius here names the enemy as Germans and Sarmatians (as he does in the *Ecclesiastical History*), but places the battle in the land of the Quadi, which may imply a coalition of sorts. His naming of Pertinax as the commander perhaps contradicts the command of Pompeianus in the letter, although the two Roman commanders may have continued to act together.

Eusebius notes that non-Christian writers refer to the incident, but do not credit it to Christian prayers, naming Tertullian and the letter cited by him as his authority. Eusebius – following Apollinarius, a Christian bishop of Hierapolis in Phrygia (modern-day Pamukkale, Turkey) in the 170s – also tells us (erroneously) that the Melitene legion was thereafter known as the Thundering Legion (*Ecclesiastical History* 5.5.4).

Orosius (7.15.9–11) gives similar detail, but writes of the small, untrained force of the Romans (7.15.10) – this seems unlikely and I have opted to place five legions at the battle. The letter appended to *The First Apology of Justin Martyr* itself offers further details, some of them contradictory to other sources:

The Emperor Cæsar Marcus Aurelius Antoninus, Germanicus, Parthicus, Sarmaticus, to the People of Rome, and to the sacred Senate greeting: I explained to you my grand design, and what advantages I gained on the confines of Germany, with much labour and suffering, in consequence of the circumstance that I was surrounded by the enemy; I myself being shut up in Carnuntum by seventy-four cohorts [*dracones*], nine miles off [*novem milliarium spatio in Cotino*]. And the enemy being at hand, the scouts [*exploratores*] pointed out to us, and our general Pompeianus showed us that there was close on us a mass of a mixed multitude of 977,000 men, which indeed we saw; and I was shut up by this vast host, having with me only a battalion composed of the first, tenth, double and marine legions [*mecum habens legionis primae, decimae, Geminae, Ferentariorum numerabile et permistam agmen*]. Having then examined my own position, and my host, with respect to the vast mass of barbarians and of the enemy, I quickly betook myself to prayer to the gods of my country. But being disregarded by them, I summoned those who among us go by the name of Christians. And having made inquiry, I discovered a great number and vast host of them, and raged against them, which was by no means becoming; for afterwards I learned their power. Wherefore they began the battle, not by preparing weapons, nor arms, nor bugles; for such preparation is hateful to them, on account of the God they bear about in their conscience. Therefore it is probable that those whom we suppose to be atheists, have God as their ruling power entrenched in their conscience. For having cast themselves on the ground, they prayed not only for me, but also for the whole army as it stood, that they might be delivered from the present thirst and famine. For during five days we had got no water, because there was none; for we were in the heart of Germany, and in the enemy's territory. And simultaneously with their casting themselves on the ground, and praying to God (a God of whom I am ignorant), water poured from heaven, upon us most refreshingly cool, but upon the enemies of Rome a withering hail. And immediately we recognized the presence of God following on the prayer – a God unconquerable and indestructible. Founding upon this, then, let us

One of the many Germanic iron shield bosses found at Vimose in Denmark. Although the surviving art does not emphasize the shield boss, they were an entirely necessary part of all shields. Some, like this one, could also be used offensively as well as performing a defensive and strengthening role for the integrity of the shield. (Odense Bys Museer/ Wikimedia/CC BY-SA 2.0)

pardon such as are Christians, lest they pray for and obtain such a weapon against ourselves. And I counsel that no such person be accused on the ground of his being a Christian. But if any one be found laying to the charge of a Christian that he is a Christian, I desire that it be made manifest that he who is accused as a Christian, and acknowledges that he is one, is accused of nothing else than only this, that he is a Christian; but that he who arraigns him be burned alive. And I further desire, that he who is entrusted with the government of the province shall not compel the Christian, who confesses and certifies such a matter, to retract; neither shall he commit him. And I desire that these things be confirmed by a decree of the Senate. And I command this my edict to be published in the Forum of Trajan, in order that it may be read. The prefect Vitrasius Pollio will see that it be transmitted to all the provinces round about, and that no one who wishes to make use of or to possess it be hindered from obtaining a copy from the document I now publish. (Justin Martyr, *Apology I*, appendix)

The detail of this letter seems entirely credible, although the number of 977,000 men opposing the Romans is not. The letter could have been based on some real information, however, perhaps adding some forged material, although it has Marcus say he was in Carnuntum and places the location of the battle in the area of the Cotini – *in Cotino* – rather than near the Quadi; this phrase was not included in the translation above. Birley (1987: 173) considered this detail feasible, as the Cotini would have needed to be punished for their shameful treatment of Paternus earlier (Dio, 71/72.3.12).

Other sources mention the Quadi, but not the Cotini. They do, however, mention that the Romans were surrounded by the enemy. The word translated as 'cohorts' above is *dracones*, 'dragons', which suggests that 74 standards opposed the Romans. We can see just such *dracones* as part of the victory trophies set upon the coins commemorating the victories against the Germanic tribes. These *dracones* are certainly possible, although it is not possible to establish how many men there were per standard (if it was ever a specific number). If it was close to the manpower of a cohort, 480 men, then 74 such units would give 35,500 men. The Latin also does not have 977,000 men at that point in the text, but *immensa et ordinata multitudine*, 'an immense and well-ordered multitude'. This fits the picture of the battle. The actual number only comes in the next sentence after the legions are enumerated (*hominum nongentorum septuaginta millium*); it could be translated as 970,000 rather than 977,000, but this is intended to contrast the two forces explicitly.

Marcus was based at Carnuntum and his having the 'first, tenth, double and marine legions' is entirely plausible, although the Latin makes this the first, tenth and *Gemina* legions and detachments of the *Ferrata*; that is, *I, X* and either (or both of) *XIII* or *XIIII* (*X, XIII* and *XIIII* all bearing the appellation *Gemina*), plus vexillations of the *legio VI Ferrata*. The picture thus drawn is of Marcus with three or four legions and vexillations of a fifth, so somewhat less than 20,000 men if with three legions, or 25,000 with four, facing a barbarian horde of almost 1 million. If we take the 74 standards as theoretically 35,500 men, then the Quadi already outnumbered the Romans.

Usually when calculating Roman armies, however, an equal number of auxiliaries are added to the number of legions. Auxiliary troops are often entirely omitted from our sources, so despite the mention of such forces in the *SHA* (e.g. *Marcus* 21.6–8), such units are not mentioned in any battle account. This doubling would bring the Roman total to 50,000 men and the Quadi would no longer outnumber such a force – but we read that the Quadi were willing to give up 50,000 captives so their total strength must logically have been greater than that. A simple solution might be to assume the Quadi had about 100,000 men, thereby outnumbering the Romans 2:1, and still representing an immense horde from the Roman perspective (perhaps the 970,000 was originally 97,000).

Interestingly, there is no mention in the letter of the *legio XII Fulminata*, the legion around which the other accounts coalesce. Eusebius refers to the Melitene legion, which was the *legio XII*, and this detail was added to Dio too. Nor is there mention of the *legio II Adiutrix*, or indeed of the new legions *II* and *III Italica* that may also have been present. The term *primae* might refer to the *legio I Adiutrix* and the translation of 'marine' might seek to include both of the *Adiutrix* legions rather than the vexillations of the *legio VI Ferrata*; the *Adiutrix* legions (the name means helper or assistant) were initially raised from marines of the Misenum and Ravenna fleets in AD 68 and 70 respectively. In my reconstruction of the battle I have included several legions (including *XII Fulminata*) because it seems unlikely a single legion would be operating independently.

Scene 71 of the Column of Marcus Aurelius shows prisoners being beheaded. Unlike the surviving sources, which emphasize the emperor's clemency and the exiling of the perpetrators of the Marcomannic Wars, there was clearly much harsher justice meted out on the frontier. Here, captive Germanic tribesmen are executed, perhaps by fellow Germanic auxiliaries in Roman service. The men wielding the swords are not armoured, but dressed as Germanic tribesmen in trousers, tunics and cloaks. The prisoners are similarly dressed – one wears only trousers – and all are bearded. (GRANGER – Historical Picture Archive/ Alamy Stock Photo)

Analysis

BARBARIAN EFFECTIVENESS

Although they were ultimately defeated – and it took the Romans ten years to do so – the various peoples beyond the Danube showed themselves to be cunning and determined enemies capable of inflicting defeats on their powerful neighbour. We might ask what the various Germanic peoples hoped to achieve; they must have known that Roman vengeance would eventually come. They cannot realistically have hoped to carve out vulnerable territory on the south bank of the Danube. Can it really have only been about raiding for plunder? Surprisingly, the answer seems to be in the affirmative; perhaps the tribes welcomed the chance to fight it out when Roman retribution arrived.

That punishment did come in 172 and subsequently. By bridging the Danube with boats, the Roman Empire demonstrated its power and determination to punish the invaders. In the face of that determined Roman campaigning in their home territories, the peoples hostile to Rome were unable to prevent defeat and the eventual garrisoning of areas beyond the Danube. Others took the opportunity to reiterate their loyalty to the empire, offering troops to fight their own erstwhile allies or their ancestral enemies. Rome's focus on the Danube frontier offered all kinds of opportunities.

That said, the wars were left incomplete at Marcus Aurelius' death and although we are told the emperor had planned the annexation of the lands of the Marcomanni as a province, we may doubt if this was his intention. We may also doubt if he could have achieved it within a year. Despite eventual defeat in 172, then 175, there was clearly still fight left in the tribes in 178 and this was not wholly extinguished by 180. Commodus' quick peace may have been condemned, but it may also have been expedient after so many years of expensive military effort. It is difficult, however, to credit that the

Germanic peoples had consciously intended to outlast a war of attrition with the Roman Empire.

The tribes did manage to coordinate with one another; we are told of the Marcomanni and Quadi working together, then the Quadi inviting the Sarmatians to invade, but those coordinated efforts did not last long and the Romans were able to defeat each tribe piecemeal in their turn, isolating allies with favourable terms and then defeating weakened alliances.

There were clearly effective commanders within the Germanic ranks even though their identities – beyond the names of some of their kings – are lost to us. The tribal warriors were able to avoid Roman garrisons, surround those that came against them and then rampage unchecked. They showed themselves capable of putting Italy under threat – the first enemy to do so for almost 300 years – and of taking towns. The warriors also showed that they could be cunning in battle – the Sarmatians and Quadi on the ice must have lured the pursuing Romans on to terrain of which they had more experience than their opponents.

What is more, it is clear many of the Germanic peoples continued to be valued and were enlisted as Roman auxiliaries. Even though the Column of Marcus Aurelius shows us the execution of prisoners, the literature, such as it is, and other surviving art places emphasis upon clemency and the new agreements between Rome and various barbarian peoples who now agreed to serve in the Roman Army. In these developments, several of the Germanic peoples got what they wanted: land to settle within the boundaries of the Roman Empire, payment and an agreement to provide troops for Rome's armies. If the Germanic people loved to wage war as Tacitus tells us they did, then by enlisting in Rome's armies they could have all the military service they wanted. Within a generation of the end of the Marcomannic Wars in 180, every freeborn occupant of the empire would be made a citizen. The *Constitutio Antoniniana* of 212 therefore probably gave those who took up land within the empire more than they could ever have hoped for. The decision to allow peoples from beyond the Roman frontier to settle in imperial territory in return for military service would, eventually, prove catastrophic for Rome during the 4th century. Those military disasters were almost two centuries off, however, and the decline of Rome's fortunes until then was gradual, even imperceptible, but the process began in earnest during the reign of Marcus Aurelius.

This bronze *sestertius* of Marcus Aurelius was minted in Rome in 177 to celebrate the Roman victory over the Germanic and Sarmatian tribes (*RIC* 3.1184). The legend records 'M ANTONINVS AVG GERM SARM TR P XXXI', and on the reverse 'IMP VIII COS III P P' and 'DE GERMANIS' in exergue. We see a variety of Germanic and Sarmatian arms, armour and shields, a *draco* and a (captured?) *vexillum*. (CNG/Wikimedia/ CC BY-SA 2.5)

ROMAN EFFECTIVENESS

The Roman forces were effective, eventually. Even though at the start of the campaigns along the Danube we seem to read of nothing in the surviving sources but unchecked incursions by various Germanic, Sarmatian and Dacian peoples, all were eventually forced back, paid off or defeated.

Accounts of the beginning of the Marcomannic Wars tell a story of imperial incompetence and the inability of Roman garrisons to deal with the invasions by various peoples. Marcus' soldiers were, however, massively outnumbered. We read that several governors and Roman Army commanders

A gold *aureus* of Marcus Aurelius minted in Rome in 176/77, commemorating both the German and Sarmatian victories. The legend reads 'M ANTONINVS AVG GERM SARM, TR P XXXI IMP VIII COS III P P, DE GERM' (*RIC* 3.362; *BMC RE* 4.737). This translates as 'Marcus Antonius Augustus, Germanicus, Sarmaticus, the power of a tribune [*tribunicia potestas*] 31 years, declared *Imperator* for the eighth time, three times consul, father of the fatherland [*pater patriae*], with regard to Germania.' The pile of captured enemy equipment shows scale armour, perhaps that of a chieftain, and various shields with different shapes and designs. Note also the *draco* standard. The Romans could discern no difference between the neighbouring Marcomanni, Quadi or Sarmatian Iazyges, and worried about members of one tribe passing themselves off as members of another. (CNG/Wikimedia/Public Domain)

were not only defeated but killed in their efforts to hold back these invasions. Events that seem to have been unmitigated disasters for the Romans, such as the defeat at Carnuntum, the capture of Opitergium and the siege of Aquileia, are glossed over by the sources.

Nevertheless, when Marcus and his commanders did finally arrive on the scene, they were able to pressure the enemy to negotiate and reaffirm their loyalty to Rome, probably in return for payment or the promise of land for settlement. This may have been all the invaders wanted, but their promises were soon broken and the Romans decided to bridge the Danube and march into enemy territory. In this the imperial forces were inexorable and the surviving sources tell us of a well-organized campaign conducted by the juggernaut of the Roman Army. The participation of several legions and multiple auxiliary units is attested to, even though there was a manpower shortage due to the plague. For the Germanic peoples, with the Roman Army campaigning in their home territory, there was nowhere to hide; facing annihilation, there was no option but to capitulate, offering men as hostages, or as troops for Rome's armies.

What is more, there are aspects to Rome's response that show it to have been relentless despite the setbacks of plague, military defeats and even adverse weather conditions. Roman troops were resilient and even when facing overwhelming odds, they seem to have kept their discipline, especially when under the eye of the emperor such as during the Battle on the Ice in 172. If the Roman forces used similar tactics to those described by Arrian in the *Ektaxis kat' Alanon* to deal with mounted Alan enemies, then in the right circumstances the Romans could hold firm and utilize the necessary impenetrable bloc of infantry in order that the missile troops behind it could shoot into the enemy ranks and ensure their defeat.

Again, when facing fatigue, thirst and being surrounded by a numerically superior enemy in the Miracle of the Rain, the Romans stood firm and, when the unexpected downpour relieved their thirst and delivered lightning strikes on the enemy, they fought on and won. This was reported as a sign of divine favour and whatever the reason behind that – Marcus' prayers, those of the Egyptian magician, Arnuphis, or even Christian prayers – it showed the Roman Army's soldiers that they enjoyed divine favour. Several of the narratives of the early 170s are concerned with the purification of the Roman Army; there was nothing so effective at dispelling any lingering idea that they were impure than the bestowal of such divine favour and victory upon the troops.

It is when the emperor himself is absent that we seem to find various armies defeated, whether at Carnuntum or during the actions undertaken by the armies of Furius Victorinus Cornelius Fronto and Marcus Vindex. That is not to say that Roman victories could only be won in the presence of the emperor. Marcus seems to have been blessed with a large number of capable subordinates, not only high-profile figures such as Pompeianus and Pertinax, but also others such as Maximianus, whom we are fortunate to know about at all. This depth of talent and experience is remarkable when we consider that the plague in Rome and within the ranks of the Roman Army must have afflicted large numbers of capable men.

Aftermath

The *SHA* tells us that Marcus 'wished to make a province of Marcomannia and likewise of Sarmatia and he would have done so had not Avidius Cassius just then raised a rebellion in the East' (*Marcus* 24.5). Responding to a rumour that Marcus was dead, Avidius Cassius mounted his usurpation attempt in 175; Marcus, 'abandoning the Sarmatian and Marcomannic wars, set out against him. At Rome there was a panic for fear that Cassius would arrive during Antoninus' absence; but he was speedily slain and his head was brought to Antoninus' (*Marcus* 25.1–2). In reality, Cassius' usurpation lasted barely three months. Marcus then showed great clemency to those who had participated in the revolt, recalling exiles and pardoning communities that had sided with the usurper. He allowed Cassius' children to live and even permitted them to inherit half of their father's estate.

Marcus had also summoned his son Commodus, born in 161, to the North to fight with him just prior to his leaving for the East (*SHA, Marcus* 22.12). According to the *SHA* (*Commodus* 2.2), Commodus assumed the *toga virilis*, usually assumed around the age of 14, on 7 July 175, so dating his presence on campaign from about 175. The first campaign in which Commodus participated, however, was that mounted in the East against Avidius Cassius.

While in the East, Marcus negotiated with the kings of Persia and showed himself very much a man to be admired. In Alexandria especially he 'conducted himself like a private citizen' (*SHA, Marcus* 26.3). From the East he travelled to Athens and was initiated into the Eleusinian Mysteries; these had been destroyed by the Costoboci so this was, in part, for propaganda purposes and not just an indication of religious reverence. From there, Marcus headed to Brundisium (modern-day Brindisi, Italy) and finally to Rome in late 176. In Rome, Marcus held a Triumph and gave a magnificent games. Commodus was made consul for 177, made co-emperor the same year and married Bruttia Crispina in 178.

A bust of the young emperor Commodus, as he may have appeared when he came to the throne in 180 at the age of only 19. He immediately made peace in the North, a decision roundly condemned in the sources. (J. Paul Getty Museum/Wikimedia/No restrictions)

Only after all these distractions did Marcus turn his attention to the Marcomannic Wars once more. The *SHA* states that he 'then turned his attention to completing the war, in the conduct of which he died. During this time the behaviour of his son steadily fell away from the standard the Emperor had set for himself' (*Marcus* 27.9). Here, the author of the *SHA* sets the pattern for the life of Commodus that would follow. He would be depicted as a 'bad' emperor, to contrast entirely with his father. The *SHA* states that for 'three years thereafter he [Marcus] waged war with the Marcomanni, the Hermunduri, the Sarmatians, and the Quadi, and had he lived a year longer he would have made these regions provinces' (*Marcus* 27.10). Dio also makes the claim that if Marcus had lived longer he would have 'subdued the entire region' (71/72.33). It is difficult to assess whether this summary was accurate, however. In the *SHA* (*Commodus* 2.5) we are given more detail and the campaign against Avidius Cassius, time spent in the East and subsequent return occupied Marcus' time from mid-175 until 178. Commodus and Marcus departed for the North again only in early August 178.

Dio tells us (71/72.20.1–2) that 20,000 Roman troops were stationed in the territories of the Marcomanni and Quadi. The Quadi were 'unwilling to endure the forts built to keep watch over them' (Dio, 71/72.20.2) and attempted to migrate, but Marcus learned of their intention and prevented the move. At the same time, 3,000 Naristi – those perhaps defeated by Valerius Maximianus – settled in Roman territory (Dio, 71/72.21). There may well have been a Roman plan to add these territories to the empire as provinces. The *SHA* suggests as much, and a medallion was issued in Commodus' and Marcus' name calling them *propagatores imperii* ('extenders of the empire') (Birley 1987: 253–55).

The *SHA* then records that shortly before his death in March 180, Marcus summoned Commodus and encouraged him 'not to think lightly of what remained of the war' (*Marcus* 28.1). As soon as he was emperor, however, Commodus dismissed his father's advisers and 'abandoned the war which his father had almost finished and submitted to the enemy's terms, and then returned to Rome' (*SHA, Commodus* 3.5). Nevertheless, he celebrated a Triumph in Rome in October that year. Herodian tells us (1.6) that Commodus abandoned the Marcomannic Wars against the advice of his father's *consilium* (council), especially Tiberius Claudius Pompeianus, one of Marcus' most trusted commanders and Commodus' brother-in-law. Pompeianus had married Lucilla, Commodus' sister and Verus' widow, just prior to Marcus' departure for Pannonia in 170. This negative summary may not tell the whole story, however, and the account in Dio (72.2–3) is more complimentary. There is also evidence of ongoing fighting against the Buri at least as late as 182 (*CIL* 3.5937). Nevertheless, the war was abandoned and the tribes across the Danube would cause almost incessant trouble for the Roman Empire over the next three centuries.

BIBLIOGRAPHY

Sources

Our major source for the Marcomannic Wars is the senator **Cassius Dio** (or Dio Cassius), born *c*.155, who wrote a Roman History (*Romaike Historia*) in 80 books. Dio's work is, unfortunately, highly fragmentary and for most of it we rely on epitomes made in the 11th and 12th centuries (by the monk John Xiphilinus and the historian John Zonaras respectively), including books 71 and 72 in which the history of Marcus' wars are recounted. It is unclear from which book some of the material is actually excerpted, so I have used 71/72 in the citations.

The historian **Herodian** (*c*.170–240) wrote a *History of the Empire from the Death of Marcus*, which begins in 180 and continues to 238.

Also helpful are other eyewitnesses to Marcus' reign such as the satirist **Lucian of Samosata**. Most important of these is Lucian's life of Alexander of Abonoteichus, founder of an important cult and oracle. Another contemporary who offers insights is Marcus' rhetoric tutor, **Marcus Cornelius Fronto**, who kept up a correspondence with his imperial student until his death in the late 160s.

Marcus Aurelius' own *Meditations*, written during 169–80, is a useful source for the insight it gives us to Marcus himself, particularly from the perspective of Stoic philosophy.

The *Germania*, the ethnographical treatise written by the historian **Cornelius Tacitus** in AD 98, offers a useful summary of the Roman view of the Germanic peoples and the relations between them.

Another treatise that proves to be immensely helpful is the *Ektaxis kat' Alanon* ('Deployment Against the Alans'), written by the historian **Arrian of Nicomedia**, who lived into the early years of Marcus' reign. Arrian had been a field commander of Roman troops and his detailed record of how he drew up his army in *c*.136/37 in Cappadocia against an Alan incursion is the best document we have from any period revealing how a Roman Army deployed in the field. **Hyginus**, or Pseudo-Hyginus, wrote a treatise on the Roman legionary camp under Hadrian (the *Liber de munitionibus castrorum*); it too is of great help.

We are also aided in our task by archaeology, numismatics and epigraphy; in some cases – such as the commander Valerius Maximianus, the commander of the *legio II Adiutrix* at Laugaricio, who is not mentioned in any literary account – we gain remarkable insights.

Many later historians include accounts of Marcus' wars and we can use them, at least in part, to build our picture. The *Historia Augusta* or *Scriptores Historiae Augustae* (often abbreviated to just *HA* or *SHA*) was a collection of biographies of emperors from Hadrian to Numerianus (so AD 117–284). Six different authors are named, but it was probably written by a single author living in the early 4th century AD, or perhaps during the reign of Theodosius I (r. 379–95). Despite the source apparently quoting official documents, it is possible that much of the work was invented.

The brief history of Rome, the *Breviarium*, written by **Eutropius** in 369 is useful but understandably brief. The *Getica* or *The Gothic History* of **Jordanes** (6th century AD) also looks back to Marcus' wars in his survey of the history of the Goths. **Ammianus Marcellinus**, writing in the 380s, also gives us valuable insights.

Several of the early Christian Church fathers give us insights, too – perhaps spurious, such as **Justin Martyr** (*c*.100–65). We can also use passages in the *Ecclesiastical History* and *Chronicon* of **Eusebius of Caesarea** (*c*.260–369), although the *Chronicon* remains untranslated into English at the time of writing. The works of Gregory of Nyssa (*c*.335–95) can also be utilized, as can **Paulus Orosius** (*c*.374–420), who wrote his *Seven Books of History against the Pagans* as a history of groups of non-Christians. Other Christian authors we can use include **Themistius** (317–*c*.388) and **Jerome** (*c*.342–420).

Inscriptions and coins

AE – L'Année épigraphique, ed. Mireille Corbier, Patrick Le Roux & Sylvie Dardaine. Multiple volumes (1888–). Paris: Presses universitaires de France. An annual collection of inscriptions referenced by the year of discovery.

BMC RE – British Museum Catalogue: Coins of the Roman Empire in the British Museum. Six volumes (1923–). London: Department of Coins and Medals, The British Museum. The coins of Marcus Aurelius are found in volume 4.

CIL – Corpus Inscriptionum Latinarum. Multiple volumes (1853–). Berlin: Berlin-Brandenburgische Akademie der Wissenschaften.

ILS – Inscriptiones Latinae Selectae, ed. H. Dessau. Three volumes (1892–1916). Berlin: Weidmannsche Buchhandlung.

RIC – Roman Imperial Coinage. Ten volumes (1923–94). London: Department of Coins and Medals, The British Museum. The coins of Marcus Aurelius are found in volume 3.

Ancient works

Ammianus Marcellinus, *Rerum Gestarum Libri*, trans. C.D. Yonge (1862). London: Henry. G. Bohn.

Cassius Dio, *Roman History*, trans. E. Cary (1914–27). Nine volumes. Cambridge, MA & London: Harvard University Press.

Eunapius, *Historia* (Fragments), trans. R.C. Blockley (1983), in *The Fragmentary Classicising Historians of the Later Roman Empire*. Cambridge: Francis Cairns.

Eusebius, *Ecclesiastical History*, trans. K. Lake (Vol. 1, 1926) and J.E.L. Oulton (Vol. 2, 1932). Two volumes. Cambridge, MA & London: Harvard University Press.

Eusebius, *Ecclesiastical History and Martyrs of Palestine*, trans. H.J. Lawlor & J.E.L. Oulton (1927–28). Two volumes. London: Society for the Promotion of Christian Knowledge.

Eusebius, *The Ecclesiastical History of Eusebius Pamphilus*, trans. C.F. Crusé & H. de Valois (1897). London: G. Bell & Sons.

Eutropius, *Breviarium*, trans. J.S. Watson (1890), in *Justin, Cornelius Nepos, and Eutropius*. London: G. Bell.

Gregory of Nyssa, trans. W. Moore & H.A. Wilson (1892), in P. Schaff & H. Wace, eds, *Nicene and Post-Nicene Fathers*, Second Series, Vol. 5. Grand Rapids, MI: WM. B. Eerdmans Publishing Co.

Herodian, *History of the Empire*, trans. C.R. Whittaker (1969–70). Two volumes. Cambridge, MA & London: Harvard University Press.

Herodian, *History of the Roman Empire from the Death of Marcus Aurelius*, trans. E.C. Echols (1961). Berkeley, CA: University of California Press.

Hyginus, *Liber de munitionibus castrorum*, trans. D.B. Campbell (2018). *Fortifying a Roman Camp. The Liber de munitionibus castrorum of Hyginus.* Glasgow: Bocca della Verità Publishing.

Jerome, *Chronicon*, trans. M.D. Donaldson (1996). *A Translation of Jerome's Chronicon with Historical Commentary*. Lewiston, NY: Mellen University Press.

Jordanes, *The Gothic History*, trans. C.C. Mierow (1915). Princeton, NJ: Princeton University Press.

Josephus, *Jewish War*, trans. W. Whiston, A.M. Auburn & B.J.E. Beardsley (1895). Edinburgh: Thomas Nelson & Sons.

Justin Martyr, *Apology*, trans. M. Dods & G. Reith (1885), in Roberts, A., Donaldson, J. & Cleveland Coxe, A. (eds), *Ante-Nicene Fathers*, Vol. 1. Buffalo, NY: Christian Literature Publishing Co.

Justin Martyr, *The First Apology*, trans. D. Minns and P. Parvis (2009), in Minns, D. & Parvis, P. (eds), *Justin, Philosopher and Martyr: Apologies*. Oxford Early Christian Texts. Oxford: Oxford University Press.

Lucian, *Alexander the False Prophet*, trans. A.M. Harmon (1925), in *Lucian*, Vol. IV. Cambridge, MA & London: Harvard University Press.

Marcian, *Periplus Maris Exteri* (Periplus of the Outer Sea), trans. W.H. Schoff (1927). Philadelphia, PA: Commercial Museum.

Marcus Aurelius, *Meditations*, trans. C.R. Haines (1916). Cambridge, MA & London: Harvard University Press.

Marcus Cornelius Fronto, *Letters*, trans. C.R. Haines (1919–20). Two volumes. Cambridge, MA & London: Harvard University Press.

Orosius, *Seven Books of History against the Pagans*, trans. A.T. Fear (2010). Liverpool: Liverpool University Press.

Pliny the Elder, *The Natural History*, trans. J. Bostock & H.T. Riley (1855). London: Taylor & Francis.

Pliny the Younger, *Letters*, trans. J.B. Firth (1900). London: Walter Scott Publishing Co.

Rufinus, *Ecclesiastical History*, trans. W.H. Fremantle (1892), in P. Schaff & H. Wace, eds, *Nicene and Post-Nicene Fathers*, Second Series, Vol. 3 (*Theodoret, Jerome, Gennadius, & Rufinus: Historical Writings*). Buffalo, NY: Christian Literature Publishing Co.

Scriptores Historiae Augustae: Vita Marcus, Vita Lucius, Vita Avidius Cassius, Vita Pertinax, Vita Severus Alexander, trans. D. Magie (1921), in *Historia Augusta, Vol. I* (1921–32). Three volumes. Cambridge, MA & London: Harvard University Press.

Tacitus, *Histories*, trans. C.H. Moore (1925 & 1931). Two volumes. Cambridge, MA & London: Harvard University Press.

Tacitus, *The Agricola and Germania*, trans. A.J. Church & W.J. Brodribb (1877). London: Macmillan.

Tertullian, *Apologeticus*, trans S. Thelwall (1885), in Roberts, A., Donaldson, J. & Cleveland Coxe, A. (eds), *Ante-Nicene Fathers*, Vol. 3. Buffalo, NY: Christian Literature Publishing Co.

Themistius, *Orations*, trans. P.J. Heather & D. Moncur (2001). *Politics, Philosophy, and Empire in the Fourth Century: Select Orations of Themistius (Oration 16)*. Liverpool: Liverpool University Press.

Vegetius, *Epitome of Military Science*, trans. N.P. Milner (1993). Liverpool: Liverpool University Press.

Modern works

van Ackeren, M., ed. (2012). *A Companion to Marcus Aurelius*. London: Wiley Blackwell.

Beckmann, M. (2003). 'The battle scenes on the Column of Marcus Aurelius'. PhD thesis. McMaster University, Hamilton, Ontario, Canada.

Beckmann, M. (2011). *The Column of Marcus Aurelius*. Chapel Hill, NC: University of North Carolina Press.

Birley, A. (1987). *Marcus Aurelius: A Biography*. Revised Edition. London: Batsford.

Bishop, M.C. & Allason-Jones, L. (1988). *Excavations at Roman Corbridge: The Hoard*. London: English Heritage.

Campbell, D.B. (2022). *Deploying a Roman Army. The Ektaxis kat' Alanōn of Arrian*. Glasgow: Quirinus Editions.

Dean, S.E. (2013). 'The great Marcomannic invasion: coalition against Rome', *Ancient Warfare Magazine* 7.6: 26–33.

Elliott, S. (2020). *Pertinax*. Barnsley: Greenhill Books.

Ferris, I. (2009). *Hate and War: The Column of Marcus Aurelius*. Stroud: The History Press.

Fletcher, B. (1921). *A History of Architecture on the Comparative Method*. 6th edition. New York, NY: Charles Scribner's Sons.

Israelowich, I. (2008). 'The Rain Miracle of Marcus Aurelius: (Re-) Construction of Consensus', *Greece & Rome* 55: 83–102.

Koepfer, C. (2013). 'Marcomannic wars in Raetia: a second theatre of war?' *Ancient Warfare Magazine* 7.6: 22–25.

Kovács, P. (2009). *Marcus Aurelius' Rain Miracle and the Marcomannic Wars*. Mnemosyne Supplements, Volume 308. Leiden: Brill.

Kovács, P. (2017). 'Marcus Aurelius' rain miracle: when and where?', *Študijné zvesti Archeologického ústavu Slovenskej Akadémie Vied Nitra* 62: 101–11.

MacDowall, S. (2013). 'Legions of Marcus Aurelius: the Roman army in transition', *Ancient Warfare Magazine* 7.6: 12–16.

Moskvin, A., Wijnhoven, M.A. & Moskvina, M. (2021). 'The equipment of a Germanic warrior from the 2nd–4th century AD: Digital reconstructions as a research tool for the behaviour of archaeological costumes,' *Journal of Cultural Heritage* 49: 48–58.

Nickel, H. (1989). 'The Emperor's New Saddle Cloth: The Ephippium of the Equestrian Statue of Marcus Aurelius', *Metropolitan Museum Journal* 24: 17–24.

Parker, H.M.D. (1958). *The Roman Legions*. Oxford: Clarendon Press.

Robinson, H.R. (1975). *The Armour of Imperial Rome*. New York, NY: Charles Scribner's Sons.

Taylor, M.J. (2013). 'Scenes of brutality: The Column of Marcus Aurelius', *Ancient Warfare Magazine* 7.6: 34–38.

Webster, G. (1998). *The Roman Imperial Army of the First and Second Centuries A.D.* 3rd edition. Norman, OK: University of Oklahoma Press.

Wijnhoven, M.A. (2022). 'From the depths of the bog: clothing, arms, and armour of a Thorsberg warrior', *Ancient Warfare Magazine* 15.5: 38–39.

INDEX

References to illustrations are shown in **bold**. References to plates are shown in **bold** with caption pages in brackets, e.g. **52–53**, (54).